HOMEWORK

HOMEWORK

Grace Langdon, PH.D.
AND
Irving W. Stout, ED.D.

THE JOHN DAY COMPANY, NEW YORK

Contents

Introduction

To assess the homework situation as it presently exists it is necessary to view it against its historical background. To discover this background a survey was made of the literature pertaining to teaching method in its relation to homework since the turn of the century.

During this period, 1900 to the present, the major treatment of the subject has been in periodicals and pamphlets rather than in any treatise of book length. In books on teaching method where homework has been discussed at all the coverage has been customarily limited to a few pages.

In the survey brief examination was made of leading books published in the period 1900 to 1950 and a detailed examination of some 200 books published since 1950 in the fields of elementary and secondary education, school administration and supervision, and guidance as related to study. In the book *Helping Parents Understand Their Child's*

*School** by the authors of the present volume, a chapter of twenty-four pages was devoted to the subject; this was considerably more than was to be found in other books.

For the survey of periodicals (including pamphlets) the *Reader's Guide to Current Literature* was consulted together with the *Education Index.* Approximately 300 articles and pamphlets were read.

During the period thus surveyed from 1900 to the present, homework, or home study, as it was synonymously designated, has been a matter of concern to educators, to parents, and, one may presume, to students. Opinions as to its usefulness have veered back and forth, pro and con. Research on the subject has been and is notably lacking. The few studies made since 1900, while suggestive, have been limited in scope, of short duration, and usually of loose design.

To summarize, there was evident in the first decade of the century considerable dissatisfaction with homework as it was being carried on. In the next decade the situation worsened rather than bettered. By the 1920's a critical eye indeed was turned upon it, though there were those who rose to its defense. With the coming of the thirties and throughout that decade the chief solution offered was its abolishment. By the forties it was evident that this was impossible, and a more constructive

---

* Grace Langdon and Irving W. Stout, *Helping Parents Understand Their Child's School* (Englewood Cliffs, N. J., Prentice-Hall, 1957).

approach appeared, with some effort to offer suggestions designed to be helpful to teachers. For the most part these suggestions stopped with the statement of policy, and teachers were left to shift for themselves in working out the details of the homework they would give, the way they would give it, and the use they would make of it.

By the fifties it had become obvious that homework as part of the school picture was an accomplished fact. More attention than heretofore was turned to how to make it useful. Suggestions, however, tended to be general rather than specific. Little or no reference was made to the subject in treatises designed to prepare students for teaching. Nor was the controversy concerning its usefulness terminated, for there still appeared hints that its abolishment might be the solution for the problems involved. With the coming of the sixties the situation was little changed, though a somewhat more hopeful view was evident. More attention turned, both in the fifties and sixties, to the matter as it related to the elementary school. Prior to this, attention had been largely focused, so far as the literature was concerned, at first on the secondary school, then extended to include the junior high school. Casual mention, however, and occasional articles indicated that in practice it was by no means confined to the older students.

Throughout the period beginning with 1900 parents kept appearing in the picture either through their own statements of point of view or through questions raised and opinions expressed as to their place in the situation. Then, even as now, there persisted the contention that their lack of knowledge of new methods made their help of questionable value. Yet it was evident that they could not be ignored. Repeatedly their comments, pro and con, were mentioned in current articles, and frequently comments would appear by some parent with definite complaints to voice or point of view to express.

The attitude of parents came forcibly to the attention of the authors of the present volume during the mid-fifties. At that time interviews were being held with parents in some 900 families, not with reference to homework nor with any intention to explore their feelings about it, but rather for the stated purpose of discovering what they would like to know about their children's schools, this information to be used for preparing the book aforementioned, which interpreted school procedures.* While it had not been the intention to explore attitudes on homework, the subject came up repeatedly. It became amply evident that one of the phases of school living that parents definitely wanted to know about was homework. In more than 80 percent of the interviews this was mentioned.

Later during the first four years of the sixties the authors undertook additional interviews, including some 300 families, this time for the express purpose of discovering parent attitudes on homework. Paralleling the interviews with parents were approxi-

---

* *Ibid.*

mately the same number of interviews with teachers and with students to ascertain what, if any, variations there might be in viewpoint in the three groups.

In none of these interviews was it the purpose to gather statistical data but rather to sample opinions and feelings of persons intimately concerned with any homework program. The variations in attitude are reflected in Chapter 2 of the present volume.

Thus one comes to the immediate present. Here is a phase of schoolwork which despite criticisms, objections, and insistence on its abolishment has stayed on. Yet out of the thousands upon thousands of words that have been written about homework no treatment of the subject has emerged that can be put into the hands of teachers to help them in dealing with it or into the hands of student teachers in preparation for their teaching careers, where they will inevitably be confronted with it. Hence the present volume.

This publication in no way takes the place of the research which is so greatly needed. Rather it is intended to give specific help to teachers until and when such research is undertaken and its findings made available.

The book is based on broad teaching and administrative experience; on the expressed opinions, viewpoints, and experiences of parents, teachers, and students; on a thoughtful weighing of those opinions and experiences in light of available knowledge of child development and the learning process. Basic to all that is presented by way of suggestion and comment is the settled conviction that homework is both a necessary and a useful phase of teaching. This point of view is amplified in the first chapter. In Chapter 2 specific suggestions are given directed toward helping a teacher understand the various attitudes toward homework likely to be represented in any classroom. In succeeding chapters suggestions are offered in planning, assigning, examining, and using the homework, with a final chapter on working with the parents.

The book is designed as a handbook for teachers actively at work and as a text for students in training for teaching. The approach is from the standpoint of the basic principles governing homework procedures, with illustrations of their applications from high school through junior high and into the elementary grades. This gives the users of the book a solid groundwork of the reasons behind the principles, making possible individual variations to fit different situations. Thus it enables a teacher to move ahead with confidence based on understanding.

1

Homework Has a Useful Function

HOMEWORK as treated in this volume is taken to mean any work related to school learning done outside the classroom, outside the regular schoolwork hours, not under the immediate and direct supervision of the teacher, and presumably at home or under the jurisdiction of the home.

Throughout the discussions attention is given to homework as it relates to both high school and elementary school students. Illustrations are purposely drawn from all school levels, since in common practice it is a function of the elementary school as well as of the high school.

The student doing homework is taking his place among a vast array of other home workers. Homework is part of getting on with a job. The auto mechanic who is genuinely concerned with his work reads up on the latest methods and tinkers with cars even though the day's work is done. The musician practices hours upon end. The gardener

It is universal

does not stop gardening when he lays down his hoe but seeks information on pest controls, on soil preparation, on other provisions for optimum growing. The carpenter, leaving the day's work behind, pores over his specifications and plans, measures, studies the woods and metals to find those best fitted to his purposes. The lawyer studies his law books, keeps up-to-date on court decisions, confers with others in his profession. The salesman pores over his sales pitch and bones up on the talking points of what he would sell. The storekeeper studies the market, scans the demands of his customers, figures out attractive displays. Any person following any occupation who would do his job well and keep abreast of the times delves into homework. School homework thus takes its place in the broad context of universal work, with teachers having theirs as well as the students, a fact which is frequently overlooked by the students.

It Extends Teaching Opportunity

Today's students live in a world where limitations of time and space are being pushed back, and vistas of human knowledge are being opened up so broad that no school day can suffice to encompass them.

Some suggest meeting the problem by lengthening the school day and extending the school year with all schoolwork done at school. Someday this may take place, but presently homework provides the teaching opportunity which the school day is not long enough to furnish. Even if it *were* sufficiently long, there is something to be said for taking school learnings home and joining them to the multitude of other learnings that goes on outside the classroom.

It Provides for Individual Assimilation and Independent Work

Each student must make classroom group learnings individually his own if they are to function in the living which is peculiarly his. Homework provides opportunity for this assimilation.

It lets him take the information, ideas, and skills that have been opened up in the classroom and put them to work in his own way, fitting them into his own experiences and thoughts. This is an essential phase of learning since each student lives in the world of his own thoughts. He relates the words spoken in the classroom to the experiences he has had and interprets them in light of those experiences.

The teacher gives an assignment. The student works on it at home. He is free to experiment, to play with ideas. It is *his* homework, and he does it in his way. He finds the points where understanding is vague. He fits what he does understand into his own pattern of thinking, broadening and deepening it. He may wonder and question. He may push parts of it aside as having little meaning for him. In any case he has had the opportunity to take hold of an assignment and to do his own thinking about it.

Making facts his own

The function of homework in fostering indepen-

dent study, in refining the ways of doing it, and in
making them habitual should never be minimized.

Working on his own The student who learns in the elementary grades to
work in such a manner can attack his high school
studies without the handicap of having to learn then
how to work on his own. The same with the high
school student going on to college. Independent
work habits are essential. This is one of the fundamental purposes of homework of which a teacher
should never lose sight.

A mathematics teacher makes the point thus: "The
students who are going to college have to know
how to study independently, and there is nothing
like homework in high school, if it is properly given,
to prepare them for it." Further he says, "The students who do not go to college still need to work
independently at whatever they do. They can't
have someone stand over them all the time if they
are going to get anywhere."

It Strengthens Learnings

As a student uses in his homework the ideas,
facts, skills, and procedures which have been opened
up to him throughout the school day, these become
more firmly rooted and more securely established.

It is only as ideas are considered and reconsid-
ered that they become accepted, rejected, or set
aside for further thought. It is only as facts are put
to work that they are likely to become so established
in thought that they will remain on tap when
needed. It is only as skills are strengthened through

use that they become second nature and not something that must be thought through detail by detail each time there is call for them.

The same holds for procedures, whether it be the procedure specified for the writing of a theme, for the making of a map, or for the solving of a problem. Homework is a way of providing the drill that reinforces classroom learnings. An eighth-grade teacher puts a finger on this point in saying, "The students just have to have drill on rules of capitalization, punctuation, sentence structure, composition form, even though they have had it in the grades before, so I get it into homework." Then it was related how a choice was given among five subjects, the assignment being to write not less than 200 words on the subject of individual preference.

Rein- forcement

Drill and practice are essential to reinforce learning, and homework—wisely devised—provides a means.

There are other types of learnings which homework strengthens when thoughtfully planned and responsibly carried out, namely, the learnings involved in actually doing the work, budgeting time so that all necessary work can be done, organizing materials so that time is not wasted searching for them, and going about the work to be done without dillydallying. These are work habits that stand a student in good stead all his life, and each bit of strengthening makes more certain that they become the natural way of working.

Work habits

There is self-discipline involved here. The opportunity that homework offers for such discipline is no

Self- discipline

small part of its potential value, the self-discipline that holds attention to the work in hand despite alluring distractions, the self-discipline that leads to persistence in the face of difficulties, that indeed takes the difficulties as a challenge rather than either a threat or an invitation to discontinuance of effort.

Homework thus thought of becomes vastly more than the mere application of given learnings. It becomes learning in itself. It holds within itself potential *for* learning and strengthening *of* learning which, if a teacher recognizes and utilizes it, deepens immeasurably the effectiveness of his teaching.

It Can Open Wider Vistas

A teacher who loves teaching longs to take students beyond the task of the day out into wider vistas of thought and enjoyment. However, time is short, and requirements must be met. Even while recognizing the further possibilities of the work at hand, the students must be held to what meets curriculum requirements. There are specific learnings to be covered, and it is the teacher's job to see that they are. But what richness is opened up when those learnings are used as the starting point for exploration to which the way is pointed through some imaginative homework assignment. No telling which student, or how many, will catch glimpses of the possibilities out yonder once the way is opened.

A man who has gone far in his chosen field of

Opportunity
for
enrichment

chemical engineering tells how it was the assignments of a high school chemistry teacher that caught his interest and gave him glimpses into the possibilities of the field of work that he chose for his career.

A sixth-grade teacher compiled a list of twenty-five words from the longer list which during that year the students were supposed to learn to use correctly. Directing them to use each word in a sentence might have been a barren assignment, but it was not. This was not a barren classroom.

They had often talked about words and their root derivations; about picturesque speech; about words as the tools for communicating ideas; about the exact choice of words to accurately express what one wants to say. They had become fascinated with what could be done with words. All of the work in English was done in this effort to arouse interest in words as conveyers of thought.

An imaginative assignment

So when it came to the particular group of twenty-five words which, for several reasons, were to be studied, the teacher told them to take the list, think it over to see what ideas each word brought to mind, then write a story, a poem, a skit, a song, a letter, or a description using those words.

The students were accustomed to challenging assignments, and they rose to the occasion. What a class period it was when they brought in their productions! They had explored with words and with ideas. Through use they had strengthened their learnings about different forms of writing. They had practiced spelling. Each had responded in an indi-

Multiple practice

vidual way. Homework thus imaginatively devised
can lead into explorations students could not know
were possible.

It Encourages Digging Deeper

Just as homework thoughtfully and imaginatively
planned can lead to broader learning so, too, can it
lead to the deepening of learning. It can be the
means of stimulating satisfaction in gaining depth
of knowledge as well as breadth. It gives the opportunity for following individual interests, and
how wise a teacher is to tie homework and interests
together. The interest furnishes the drive. The homework furnishes the means for deepening the interest and bringing it to more satisfying fruition.

A third-grade group had read a series of accounts
in one of their supplementary readers about insects, about the food they eat, and about how they
Extending   live and protect themselves. They became deeply
opportunity   interested, but there was other work to be done,
and they had to go on to it. The teacher, however,
did not let the interest drop but used homework as
the opportunity for helping the children dig deeper
into the wealth of knowledge which they had only
just touched upon. Simple reference material was
made available to them to take home to read and
then to report back on to the group. Dittoed sheets
of material were prepared for them. They were en-
couraged to go to the library for further material.
The parents were told of the interest, and on

Monday mornings for a period of weeks child after child brought in insects gathered on weekends and properly housed and cared for. This was homework that helped the children dig deeper in a field of interest that could conceivably lead some of them on and on. Many a hobby has had just such a start. The very habit of digging deeply into something that is of interest, instead of being content with a superficial and fleeting glance at it, is learning in itself quite apart from the facts being gathered. Still further is the learning of *how* to dig deeply.

Leading-on possibilities

It Indicates Area of Need for Individual Help

To the alert teacher who is on the lookout for points where individual students need special help, the homework they do—if thoughtfully considered —is effective in pinpointing specific needs.

Here is one student for whom historical facts brought out in class discussions and in assigned reading still seem to hang in isolation instead of falling into place in the context of the succeeding periods of human living. Here is another who has ideas to express but who cannot seem to get them into such sentence structure as makes for comprehension on the part of the reader. Here is another whose work reveals consistent lack of understanding of some principle of problem solving brought out in class.

Needs vary

So one can go through any set of homework productions of whatever sort and put a finger on the special need of this student or that one. Thus for those who wish to use it so, homework serves as an invaluable teaching guideline. This is very different from taking homework as a perfunctory necessity or as something useful primarily for those students who show signs of falling behind in their work. It is rather taking the point of view that in the whole vast area of school learnings each student stands at a different point, that the most effective teaching is done when that point is recognized for each one, and that what is done in individual homework is revealing of individual need.

Teaching guideline (margin note)

A Link Between School and Home

Homework is one means, perhaps the only means, in a teacher's hands for reaching into the home of every student in the classroom. It is a means of communication with parents. Some may say that in high school, where one tends to think of the heavy load of homework as being concentrated, such communication is not necessary. That idea best be given second thought. The question might better be raised as to whether with *more* communication there might be fewer dropouts?

A homework assignment, whether it is given in high school or in the grades, speaks to the parents of what the teacher is trying to help the students to learn. It speaks to them of what goes on in school, of what the teacher looks upon as important. It is a factor in relationships with the parents.

A Phase of Good Teaching

Relating as it does to students' learning and contributing constructively as it can to that learning, homework becomes a means of teaching, a teaching tool. It is not something to be undertaken lightly. Homework thoughtfully planned, purposefully guided, constructively used, is an invaluable teaching aid. Homework directed toward the purposes outlined in this chapter becomes an inherent phase of good teaching. It is not extraneous to it. It is inherent in it. It is a phase of teaching to which a teacher may well give thought and direct energies toward devising and using it effectively.

A teaching aid

Its overall purpose is to serve as a means of helping students lay hold upon the learning school has to offer and to make that learning reach its highest possible effectiveness in their living. This broad definition of purpose implies that homework, as the term 'is used here, must be more meaningful than evidenced in a perfunctory assignment such as, "Read the next ten pages." It must be indicative of specific intent to strengthen, stimulate, and aid learning. As used throughout this book such intent is assumed whenever the word is mentioned.

Homework should be meaningful

It is not sufficient, however, for a teacher to merely recognize and accept this all-inclusive purpose of homework. It remains to define specific purposes which will serve as guides in planning it and carrying it forward.

No claim is made that all teachers subscribe to

the usefulness of homework as herein set forth. The only claim is that the usefulness pointed out is in-herent in homework when it is purposefully planned and used.

Teacher opinion varies

It is recognized that there are teachers who hold the honest conviction that there is little need for taking on the task of homework before junior or senior high school. Others maintain that benefits can accrue long before and that wisdom suggests the early establishment of the work habits which can be furthered through its use. Many agree that with-out homework it is an impossibility to bring into students' experience the school learnings expected. Others point to the possibility of a reevaluation of the curriculum to eliminate what they consider non-essentials that have accumulated over the years, thus leaving time for what would then be desig-nated as the essentials. This, it is said, would cut down on the necessity for the homework which they see as a burden for both students and teachers.

Meanwhile in the general run of schools home-work is expected, and teachers are confronted with the necessity of doing something about it, which is the reason for providing the guidelines offered in the chapters which follow. These are presented with the settled conviction that homework *can* be so devised and carried on as to be eminently useful.

2

Understanding Student and Parent Viewpoints

STUDENTS are the homework consumers. Here, as in all else, consumer attitude determines how far the product offered can be expected to reach its potential usefulness.

Inextricably interwoven into every student's point of view and affecting his attitude toward homework are the points of view of his parents. These are evidenced in verbal comment, in the way homework facilities are provided or not provided, in the degree and nature of any help that is given, in the respect or lack of respect accorded to it.

It is only as a teacher views homework from the student angle and the parent angle that he can hope to have an understanding that will contribute to making it a fit instead of a misfit.

The Students

Presented herewith are varied points of view which a teacher may reasonably assume are likely to be represented in greater or lesser degree in the average classroom.

These have been gleaned over a long period of time from comments of students when asked directly their feelings about homework; from remarks overheard as students have gathered in groups; from telephone conversations recounted by parents when homework time approached; and significantly from the obvious effort put into (or not put into) homework assignments and from the ensuing results.

Generally Accepted as Necessary

"Sure you've got to have homework," said a fifteen-year-old boy in second year high school. "If you didn't you'd get out of school only knowing about half of what you ought to, and all that good time would be wasted and no telling when you'd **"You have** catch up. But they don't need to pile it on too **to have it"** heavy as if we had to learn all there is to know before we get out of high school." Reasonable, realistic point of view, isn't it? In back of the fussing and griping that one hears and despite the wishing that it did not have to be, one can assume that the students know full well that school hours are not long enough nor numerous enough to encompass the learning to be done.

Nor is all of the acceptance of homework a reluctant acceptance. One finds those for whom **Some** some assignment has sparked an interest that car-**enjoy the** ries them beyond the point of necessity into volun-**learning** tary searching for facts or further exploration of the possibility opened up by the requirement, or has added practice in the achievement of some skill.

There are those, too, who delight in the learning that the homework opens up, who derive great satisfaction from the feeling of accomplishment that digging into it brings. "I wouldn't have my teachers know it, nor the other kids," said a high school senior, "because I gripe about it with them. We all do, but I get a big charge out of doing it so that I turn in a good paper."

Can a teacher, then, assume that behind the griping that goes on there lies acceptance in general? Probably so. It is not that the young people necessarily reason it out as did the one in the first illustration above. It may be that the habit of acceptance grows from the time of school entrance, an acceptance that, shall we say, accumulates.

The junior high schooler knows that high school means homework. He takes it for granted. The upper grade school boy or girl knows that he will have more as he moves on than he has now. It is a part of growing up. He accepts it. The middle grade children see the bigger ones taking books home and hear them talking about homework. They take it as part of what to expect, and so they accept what the teacher asks of them. The younger ones take to it naturally and get under way with it before they even know that it is homework. Witness the first grader who rushes home with his cherished reader under his arm, ready to read over and over, to anyone who will listen, the lesson of the day. It is schoolwork done at home, and it is the beginning

A habit
of
acceptance

of acceptance that schoolwork and homework go together. It is voluntary homework, and we point to it as the first little beginning of that acceptance. It is the foundation for later acceptance.

This is not to imply that all voluntary homework is confined to little children. Mention has already been made of the high schooler who reaches beyond the assignment to something which that assignment has opened up. Thirteen-year-old Jim was doing voluntary homework when he spent the major portion of a Saturday drawing orbital maps of a succession of space flights. These correlated with the class discussions in social studies but were not assigned nor even suggested by the teacher. "Sure," he said when queried about it, "lots of us think up things like that, and it's a kind of surprise to the class."

Some is done voluntarily

Within any group of students one can expect to find acceptance of homework on the part of many with the degree of acceptance varying.

It Can Be a Great Nuisance

There is no doubt that students often look upon homework as a nuisance, and one may as well admit that by its very nature that characteristic is inherent in it.

As a first-year high school student stated it, "As long as there is school and you are in it, you'll get homework, and you've got to live with it, but it interferes with your personal life in a big way."

Another echoes the sentiments. "I know you've

got to have it, but you have to miss a lot of life for it like TV and dates, and it cuts down something awful on the visits you can have over the telephone with friends."

Whatever the age of the student the nuisance angle is likely to play its part in his feelings, more with some than with others, oftener with some than with others. Between the extremes of those who see it as a nuisance *all* of the time and those who see it as a nuisance only *some* of the time lie those who see it thus on occasion but not always. And usually there are some who label it a nuisance publicly but privately look upon it as not so bad as might be. All these points of view are likely to be represented in any classroom at any time. They are there for a teacher to take into account and to understand.

An inter-ference aspect

It Depends on What Kind It Is

Students are usually perceptive in laying a finger on what makes them shy away from homework and go into gripe sessions about it.

"Homework that is strictly on the text," says a third-year high school student, "is for the birds. It gets awfully boring but when it's some kind of science project or creative writing or even problems you have to make up to illustrate something, it's not so bad, but just reading the text and then telling in class what it said is awful, and I don't see any sense in it, if you know what I mean."

Want a challenge

Yes, one knows what he means. He is asking for challenge, for a chance to think, for an opportunity to use some individuality. "With the kind of homework you prefer, would you still gripe?" he was asked.

His reply was honest and forthright. "Yes," he said, "I would, but I wouldn't really have much to gripe about, and most of the time I wouldn't except you know when we all get to talking and you're all griping." Lots of homework griping is just that—chiming in with what the others are saying.

"The kind of homework I go for," said another high schooler, this one a senior, "is the kind that you've got to do, not the kind you can get by without doing." Then he explained what he meant. "In lots of the assignments," he said, "If you're smart you can skim chapters and get enough high spots to recite. Then if you wave your hand around, most teachers think you've got it and ask the ones that don't wave their hands. That way you really don't have to do much of it. But when they give you something that you've got to do some brainwork on, you respect it even if you don't like it, and you feel better about doing it."

A kind one can respect

Repeatedly students speak their dislike of and lack of respect for the assignment to "read the next ten pages and be ready to discuss it in class." They tell how the ones who "talk off the tops of their heads" fool the teacher into thinking they are "something special" and how the ones who are glib with asking some high-sounding questions can get a teacher to answer them while the others sit and watch the minutes tick off.

Let no one think that it is only the older, more

mature students who want homework that is vital, not dull; challenging, not boring.

Fifth-grader Donald and next door neighbor Lorna Lee, both in the same classroom, came home on the last day of the school year with two booklets in their hands, eager to show them, obviously proud and pleased. One was *History, 1963–64*. The other was *Stories, Poems, and Reports*. Each carried the student's name. Each was a compilation of homework assignments for the year, the one in history, the other in language. Each student in the classroom had similar books. Each had designed the covers which were made in art class. The work was something of which to be justly proud. Had all the students done as well as these two? No. The teacher said there was the usual range from very good to only passing fair. The point is it was homework which had been given dignity, and the students respected it.

Give dignity to it

The booklet on *History 1963–64* was the story of events of the year worth chronicling, school events of note, local events of significance, national events of importance, world events of great moment. Homework assignments had included the continued search for accounts of events that met the criteria developed in class discussions; then the final selection and arranging of those that best met the criteria. There was the writing up of events not found in the papers but worthy of note and the condensation of accounts decided to be too long or too detailed for inclusion per se. Again it was homework the students respected.

"I always thought that history was something that happened a long time ago," said one, "but it's going on every day, and the teacher told us that whatever is in the papers is history already, but it isn't all of it important, and we have to think about whether it is or not."

Students have their own ideas about the kind of homework they respect, the kind into which they are willing to put effort. A teacher does well to pay due attention to those ideas.

But how can a teacher know the kind of homework that will call forth constructive effort? By talking with different students with the honest desire to see into their thinking. By listening with open mind to what they have to say without putting any defensive argument or self-justifying explanations in the way. It can be downright revealing when students are convinced that a teacher genuinely wants to know what they think.

The Way Homework Is Given
Makes a Big Difference

Over and again high school students speak their dislike of assignments that are "thrown at us after the bell rings and we've got to start gathering our things up for getting to the next class." Just as unpopular are the assignments in which students are left to guess what is wanted—just the bare assignment given, no preparatory comments, no lead into the subject matter, no explanation of what is expected, no suggestion of possible approaches.

A social studies student tells of an assignment that was just the opposite of those that leave students uncertain and in the air. It was an assignment for which the young people had great respect and into which they plunged with enthusiasm. It entailed interviews with local government officials. They explored and practiced interview techniques. They decided what type of information they wanted to gather. The assignment was given to them in a way that made them feel confident and at ease. They were not left to flounder. Neither were they so circumscribed as to leave no room for initiative.

They want certainty

In high school or grade school the same principles apply. The way an assignment is given makes a big difference in the students' feelings about it. When it is presented so that students can approach it with confidence, when they know what it is all about, and when they have some idea of how to go about it, it is easily understandable that they will look more favorably on the assignment than when they are left to flounder and guess at what is expected.

Students Want to Know How
They Do on Homework

From senior high school, through junior high school, right on down through all the grades the story is the same. The students want to know how their homework efforts measure up.

"You want to know how you did on it," they say.

This is one comment that one can be sure is well-nigh universal. To one with keenly listening ears students are asking for more than a grade. They are asking for recognition of the fact that they did the work. They are asking for assurance that the teacher knows what they did. They are asking that their work be respected enough to be evaluated, not thrown into the discard file nor shoved aside as of little moment. How it raises the ire to feel that what was given was busywork.

They want it looked at

"I'm always suspicious," said a high school senior, "that [the homework] is being given but not looked at, and even when I see a grade on it I'm not sure it's been read unless there are some comments." Then he told how his suspicion had its roots in an experience which he had in the fifth grade. He went back after school one day to get a forgotten sweater. There in the wastebasket he saw all the homework papers that had been handed in that morning, his own among them.

Not the grade but the recognition

Students are keen enough in their feelings about the evaluative aspects of homework. "I don't care so much about the grades I get on it," said one student, "but it lets you know what you better look out for in exams if they put on something that lets you know where you got off wrong."

One could never expect to fathom all the viewpoints of students of different school levels on the matter of homework evaluation. One thing one can be sure of. It is the nature of students to want attention paid to the work done.

Whatever the varied viewpoints of the students

with whom he works, a teacher must deal with them all as he dispenses the homework which presumably he has thoughtfully devised to help them strengthen their learnings.

They know well enough that they must have it. A high school girl points to the inevitability of it in saying, "Dad had it. Mom had it. Grandpop had it. I suppose Grandmom did. I've got it. I guess likely my children will have it. So you might as well take it and like it."

Yes, but the taking can be more useful and the liking more probable if the teacher has an eye out for the shrug that speaks volumes or the glance that tells as much as words or the comments that well up out of inner feelings. Get homework geared to feelings of acceptance, and learning is on its way. But for those feelings of acceptance to come uppermost, those of nonacceptance have to be cleared away. And in either case a teacher must know what generates the acceptance or the nonacceptance. So—we say—be alert to their feelings.

Alertness to their feelings

The Parents

Many times a teacher forges ahead with homework with no particular thought about the parents who have to live with it as surely as do the students. This is usually no intentional neglect but rather a lack of recognition of the vital part parents play in homework, or an uncertainty about how to make contact with them on it, or a feeling that pressure of many duties leaves no time for doing it. Whatever the reason it is shortsighted to neglect parents' opinions and feelings, for they are a vital factor in the student's performance.

Just as one can expect variation in student points of view, so one can expect variation in those of parents.

"They Need It"

"I don't trust the school," says a father of five, "that doesn't see to it that there is homework. There's got to be. The school can't do it all unless they keep them there from daylight to bedtime. Lots of teaching has to be done at home or it doesn't get done, and something is wrong if a teacher doesn't give them work to bring home."

Those who hold to this point of view, that homework is necessary, cite varied reasons other than that which this father mentions, such as putting out-of-school time to good use, the opportunity offered for establishing good work habits, the practice it gives in independent study.

A father with seven children scattered from one in kindergarten to a senior in high school says, "It's the idea of digging in and working at it. That is what I want them to get, and homework makes them do it. School is their business, and you never get anywhere with any business unless you dig in. I say let them all have homework and plenty of it."

Homework is necessary

A teacher can feel confident that parents are usually greatly concerned that their children and young people shall learn, and generally speaking homework is tied into their thinking as associated with and essential to learning.

But There Are Dissenters

There are those, however, who maintain that school learning is the teacher's business and not the parents'. Others object that homework interferes with home chores. Still others point to the student's need for relaxation instead of more schoolwork.

Often one runs into the objection typified by the mother who says, "Why should they bring work home from school? I've got enough to do, and it ends up with my doing a lot of it myself or riding herd on them while they do it, and I've got enough without that. They don't want it, and I don't either."

Some don't
want it

Sometimes parental dissent is tied to objections to a type of homework which they disapprove; to an amount which they consider excessive; or to the way of assigning it which leaves the student in the dark as to what is wanted or how to go about it.

Such dissent raises questions as to homework practices. It points to the possibility that practices in planning and assignment might bear close scrutiny with a view to improvement. Dissent is not to be brushed off lightly; nor is the fact to be ignored that it is likely to be represented in any classroom.

The Kind Makes a Big Difference

What kind of homework do parents approve? What kind do they disapprove? Do they tend to approve and disapprove the same kinds? No. But there are some common denominators that serve as pretty sure guides.

A father of six puts his finger squarely on one type commonly approved. He says, "The children do not mind homework when it has meaning and is interesting, and we say hurrah when one of them hits a teacher that knows how to make it interesting, because while we still have to prod them, we don't have to drive them to get it done."

Tied to interest

It is natural for parents to take the student's interest as one measure of the usefulness of the homework. When he is interested, he digs in without the necessity of breaking through a wall of resistance before getting at it. Nor, if he is interested, does he see the work he is doing through a mist of dislike, resentment, rebellion, or boredom. It is a boon for all concerned when homework is tied to interest and challenge.

See it as helping them

Not only does interest take the student through any one given assignment but it also tends to keep alive an interest in school and in learning. A father speaking of this says, "Our boy's sixth-grade teacher somehow got those kids to see that their homework was to help them learn and got them so interested in learning that they didn't fuss even about the drill homework because they saw how it was helping them."

While not all parents would thus express themselves, any teacher can assume that homework is likely to get parental approval when it is done willingly and with interest. Whether or not they see it as conducive to learning, they definitely see it as more comfortable than when its accomplishment comes only through battle.

It must always be borne in mind that children begin to get their ideas about homework while in the grades. Likewise parents get their ideas about it firmly set long before those children get to high school or junior high school, where it is commonly taken to have its greatest importance.

Tied in with other activities

A father speaking of the attitude of high school twins in the family said, "We were lucky with the teacher the boys had in the second grade. She was always getting homework tied up with their running around and exploring. You'd be surprised how much they would find to take to school to talk about. She'd give them different things to look for, like seedpods, or bugs, or different kinds of traffic signs, or different kinds of houses on the block, but she'd tell them to come and tell about anything else they saw, too." Then he told how "she would sometimes have them looking for all the words they could find anywhere, on signs, in newspapers, anywhere that began or ended in a certain way." He ended his comments with, "The way I see it, homework means more to them when it is mixed up with all the things they are thinking about anyway."

It is easy enough to see why parents would look with favor on homework that is devised to tie in with compelling and absorbing out-of-school interests. It keeps all of the living going along together, each part of it furnishing impetus for the others.

There is one type of homework which a teacher

No busy-work

can expect parents to be practically unanimous in disapproving. That is the busywork type, the kind that fills in time with little evident purpose. Hear what a mother says about this. "I call it nothing in the world but busywork when they have to do three pages of problems all alike, and if they could do the first one, why should they have to do the others over and over?"

A father of a girl in junior high school tells how the teacher had told the students to copy certain material on the life and work of a writer they were studying. The father asked the girl what she thought about the material she had copied. Her reply, he said, "took me by the ears."

She said, "Don't be silly, Daddy. We aren't supposed to think about it. We're just supposed to copy it." He said, "That is what I call busywork, and I do not approve of it."

Disapproval of busywork homework ties in directly with the approval of homework with purpose.

Ideas Vary on the Emphasis

Mention has already been made of homework that challenges interest to the point where parents do not have to do more than mild prodding, if any, to get it done.

There is another angle to the kind of homework that is given, and here one finds less agreement than on the above point of challenge.

There are parents who lay great stress on memorization, memorization of poems, memorization of historical facts in their chronological sequence, memorization of mathematical and scientific formulas, memorization of various types of general information. Says one father speaking for many, "It is good to have your mind filled with things you have memorized so that you don't have to run to a book every time you want to know something."

Memorization or creative thinking

Others say, "Why have them memorize a lot of stuff when they'd better be spending their time on learning where to go to find it if they want it?" Still others, like a mother of five, speak for stress on thinking. She says, "I don't want a lot of time spent on memorization. I want our children to learn to think, and I am glad when they have homework that demands it."

Contrary to this are those who want the thinking and creative work to be done at school. "Homework is for drill on the stuff they are learning," says a father. "It's not for thinking up a lot of new stuff that means we have to work on it as hard as they do."

Some favor drill

All of these comments point to one fact: that in any classroom, in back of the students are parents who have their own ideas about what the homework should or should not be.

Homework Is Not for Punishment

Here is one point of common agreement. "Why," parents ask, "make a child abhor homework by making it a vehicle for punishment?"

A mother tells of her indignation and of family

disgruntlement over an assignment given as punishment for the misbehavior of a few when the teacher left the classroom momentarily. The task was to look up at home and bring to school seventy-five words synonymous with or descriptive of misbehavior.

"Such a performance," the mother said, "defeats the whole purpose of homework because it is so unfair, and there is no learning in it unless it is the learning to hate anything called homework."

Defeats
the
purpose

The point is often made that when homework is meted out as punishment, it builds up resentment that blocks learning, and that one piece of work thus given so upsets a student as to prevent his settling down to any of the other assignments that may have no punitive purpose in them. It accomplishes nothing in the right direction (that of learning) and much in the wrong (that of hating the whole thing).

Begin Homework Early—Wait Until Later

The question of when homework should begin strongly evokes divergent viewpoints.

High
school

"Wait until high school," say some, "or at any rate until junior high." "Begin it as soon as they start to school," say others, "and get them accustomed to the idea."

Not all would feel as strongly on this point of beginning early as a mother who tells of making up homework for her second grader because she felt he should have it even though the teacher did not give it. In fifth grade a girl came home with consistently poor grades but with *A* for effort. The mother thought the girl needed some homework to expend some good solid effort on. She insisted that she have it. Grades improved.

No, early in grades

For the most part few are likely to advocate *no* homework before junior high. Usually the argument simmers down to the idea that it is probably best to get started by the fourth or fifth grades in order to establish the habit of taking some responsibility for independent work. This with the assumption that it will increase in difficulty with each succeeding grade. But—always there are qualifications.

Probably in middle grades

Homework May Be Overdone

A mother of two high schoolers, in talking to a teacher, entered a vigorous complaint. She said, "You folks ought to get together and split up the homework by nights. *You* give some and five others do the same, and the kids are up all night if they get it done, and if they don't they are in trouble. It's an abuse of parents. We have to dig in and help, or they'd never get to bed."

Too much the same night

The complaint is frequent that students do not have enough time for recreation; that there is so much homework they cannot lend a hand with home chores; that they have to forego outside activities such as music lessons or dancing lessons; that if the boy has a paper route or some other work or

Interferes with other things

the girl baby-sits, getting homework done means "staying up until all hours, and then in the morning it's a job to get them up."

A father who takes a realistic view of the matter says, "It's hard for parents to know whether there is too much or not. It depends on the kid. Maybe he goofs off in school and that's why he has so much to do at home. Maybe he sits and looks at his books at home, and it seems as if he has too much, but it wouldn't be if he got down to work. How's a parent to know?"

Hard for parents to know

It Affects Family Living

Thus far nothing has been said except by implication of the effect of homework on family living. This cannot be neglected by the teacher who would understand the viewpoint of both students and parents. The impact is far greater than many realize. The moment a homework assignment comes in the door it becomes a part of family living. It could not be otherwise. A teacher's realization of the points of impact gives insight that can be had in no other way into the reactions of the students.

There is the problem of a place where the homework can be done. Here is a mother who says, "Because of lack of space in our house and five of them with homework, most nights it is done all over the place, in the living room, the dining room, the kitchen, wherever thay can find a spot." Then she told how there are favorite places and how the jockeying for these begins the minute the first one comes

Must be fitted in

in from school and plumps his books down with,
"Now don't anyone move them, this is my place.
I got here first."

But suppose there is less space than these five
have to jockey over—less space and just as much
homework? It still must be fitted into the things
others in the family are doing, fitted into the time
required for all of the family activities. Sometimes
it is a tight fit.

A mother who works to support her family says,
"The children (three) have to do lots of the house-
work because I don't get home until six, and it takes
some tight planning to get everything out of the
way so they can do their schoolwork."

The timing of the homework is often inconvenient, the day of the week that it is given, the date it is
due, the time between the two. Many parents object to weekends as an inconvenient time for homework to pile up. Assignments due on Monday present a problem if the family is one for weekend
company, if weekends are used for trips, or if this is
the time set aside for dancing and music lessons.
Again and again homework is cited as being inconvenient because of its interference with home
chores. There are just so many hours, and if those
are needed for homework, other things get left out.
A father on a farm says, "The more homework the
boys have, the more barn and yard work I have to
do, and in a busy season it's upsetting; but homework comes first, so they do it and I do their work."

One of the inconveniences frequently mentioned
is the curtailing of the parents' use of TV and radio

Sometimes
it's
inconvenient

in the interests of quiet for homework. "It's a funny thing," says a father, "that when they have some program on that they want, they maintain that they can work better with it going, but just let me put on a program that I want, and they can't work because of the noise."

"The biggest inconvenience that homework makes for us," said a mother, "is having to get the table cleared for them to work." She and Dad like to linger over their last cup of coffee, but when there is homework, there is no time for it because the kitchen table where they eat is the only place in their small house for it to be done.

At no point is the impact of homework on family living more direct and more significant than in the actual doing of it. How do parents feel about giving direct help? There are those who maintain that it is the child's or young person's duty and that it is up to them to do it. There are those who see their role as helping when an obstacle looms up that seems too big a hurdle. There are some who tell of working right along on the assignment and others who check it at the end. As for those who do the work in order to insure a good grade—one does hear of some of these.

Parents speak of helping in other ways, such as providing reference materials, encyclopedias, dictionary; making opportunities for trips; discussing current affairs, and the like.

But—as a mother said in telling of doing some of these things, "We just do them, but we don't know how much it really helps with their assignments.

Parent help needed

We think it must help some to have a fund of information at hand and a variety of experiences to draw on."

How helpful it would be for a teacher to be able to discover the thoughts and feelings of the parents of each student about homework in general and that of their boy or girl in particular! How enlightening it is when even the beginnings of such a discovery are made!

Those thoughts and feelings reach back into the parents' own experiences as students. They relate to their ambitions for their children. A father says, "When I see them sitting there in the evening with their problems and their spelling and their high school themes, I think to myself, 'That's what I am working so hard for, so they can have it,' and if it wasn't for the homework they wouldn't get so much out of it, so I keep a pretty close eye on it, and I don't let them get by without doing it."

Not all look so deeply into homework. Whether they look deeply or skim the surface, the teacher at any school level does well to look past the students in the classroom to the parents at home to discover their attitudes. Only so can there be understanding of student attitude, and only with some understanding of student attitude can homework be fully effective.

3

Planning the Homework

THERE are definite and specific techniques involved in making homework useful. There is nothing obscure nor difficult about them. They are based on the same general principles that underlie all good teaching. This is equally true whether the homework involves high school students and their learning or elementary students and their learning.

It is recognized that different school systems have varying policies regarding homework; some setting forth specific requirements concerning it, others leaving it to the individual teacher's discretion, some taking no definite position on it. A teacher in any given system must, of course, be familiar with the policies of that system and must work in accordance with them.

It should be understood that all suggestions offered in the chapters that follow are predicated on the considered conviction that homework is a phase of good teaching and is both necessary and desirable beginning in the elementary grades and extending through the high school. Thought of thus, it becomes something in which every teacher does well to become adept and proficient.

Planning

Planning homework is as individual a matter as every other phase of good teaching. However there are general aspects of planning which every teacher who would make use of homework must consider. Each must select the kinds to be used for different purposes. Each must make the assignments. Each must consider the use to be made of the work when it is done. Each must make some evaluation of it (or decide to consign it to the wastebasket unevaluated, and of this beware). Each must cope with student and parent reactions, known or unknown. Though approach and method may and should be individual, there are basic considerations which serve as guidelines, whatever the particular situation may be.

The first of these is that homework, if it is to be useful, must be planned. There is no alternative. There is no room for hit-and-miss superficiality in homework. Respect for the students, consideration for their learning, concern for the work habits being put into use, all point to the necessity for planning homework and planning it thoughtfully.

Kinds of Planning

There are two kinds of planning to consider; overall long-range planning and daily specific planning. The overall planning takes into account the students and their general abilities; the curriculum material one is expected to cover; the policies of the given school concerning homework; and one's own point of view on it.

Whatever the local situation may be, it is natural (and eminently useful) for a teacher to plan ahead for the school year; thinking how to use homework; the part homework can play in the students' learning; the variety that can be used considering the specific situation; the general nature of the assignments one sees as useful; the possible ways of utilizing the homework as teaching material; the ways of evaluating it so that it eventuates in added learning.

Overall planning

This is general overall planning which furnishes the background for daily specific planning. It never takes the place of daily planning but rather clarifies one's basic philosophy as it applies to the homework situation in a given classroom and so provides the only sound basis for day-to-day plans.

Daily planning

The daily planning, if homework is to achieve its potential usefulness, takes into account where the students stand in their learning in the specific area to which the homework applies; and the next step which they are ready to take. This is planning which considers the students as individuals, with thoughtful assessment of the special help each needs in order to forge ahead. It is planning that takes into account the progress being made in covering specified curriculum material, that looks realistically at the need for drill, and with appraising eyes considers evidences of need for practice and more practice. It is in this daily planning that the teacher takes cognizance of the learning to be accomplished and of the homework that will help do it.

What Is the Purpose?

There is no point to homework unless it does something for learning. That means that a teacher who plans it thoughtfully begins with the query, "What do I want homework to accomplish?"

Reference here is not to the general purposes already discussed, such as learning to work independently, budgeting time so that all can be done, strengthening good study and work habits, and the like. These purposes are always in the background. *General purpose*

The specific purpose of any one proposed assignment may be to aid the students in becoming familiar with the form for a theme in English; to provide meaningful practice in applying principles that guide the choice and development of main points in reviewing a book or magazine article; to get certain historical facts in perspective so that they are not isolated bits of information; to become proficient in spelling words commonly needed; to gain skill in using a certain type of reference material; to get rules for punctuation firmly fixed in the mind; to discover some scientific fact; or to give practice in solving a certain type of mathematical problem; and so on. *Specific purpose*

Specific planning for day-to-day homework requires thought about the students and their individual progress in relation to the required curriculum materials. It takes thought about their individual abilities; about the resources of the school and community which one can draw upon; about the different types of homework that can be devised to suit the purpose at hand. Always the starting point for the planning, no matter what the grade level of the students, must be—What purpose do I want this homework to accomplish?

A Range for Choice

With all the possibilities for choice in the types of homework there is no need to let it become monotonous, boring, subject to the charge of "the same old thing." Activities to which students commonly gravitate outside of school offer suggestions to an alert teacher for homework that follows the line of natural interest and so makes use of inner motivation without the necessity for overcoming initial inertia in getting it done. Again, as mentioned previously, illustrations relate to all school levels since homework pertains to all.

OBSERVING

Students in the primary and elementary grades on through seniors in high school are keen observers. Why not apply this skill to science, history, geography, or language arts, whether it be high schoolers needing to select a subject for public speaking or first graders learning to put ideas together in telling something of interest to the group?

Possibilities are endless. Think of the classroom discussions that can emanate from out-of-school observations, of the themes those observations can furnish for stories, poems, creative writing of all kinds, of the scientific information that can be gathered. The teacher who is keen to note what the students are observing has at hand a wealth of possibilities to draw upon for homework assignments.

COLLECTING

What a motivating force to tie in with homework in almost any school subject! Through an imaginative homework assignment a sixth-grade teacher stimulated collection of historical data relating to the local community. It carried the students over a period of weeks. Material gathered included both tangible objects and informational facts. It all served a useful purpose in social studies, language arts, science, and mathematics.

The point is not so much what is collected as the fact that here lies a common interest to be utilized, whether the subject be high school biology, botany, zoology; third-grade beginnings of science, or fourth-grade beginnings of art.

DISCOVERING AND RESEARCHING

Why not send students on a firsthand search for facts, for information, for know-how that ties in with what they are to cover in the curriculum instead of trusting to the books? Why not send them out to supplement their book knowledge with firsthand searching on their own? This method utilizes a natural and common interest not only to unearth useful material but to strengthen the habit of independent study.

PROBLEM SOLVING

All too often as students go on in the grades the willingness that they brought to school as little children to tackle a problem gives way to hunting for the answer in the back of the book. Homework that keeps student interest in finding the solution independently has a high usefulness. Nor need problem solving be limited to those problems that are set down in the book. There is a broader view than this to take of problem solving.

A high school homemaking teacher whose group was studying child care gave them the following problem: A girl of fourteen has to get her four-year-old sister and three-year-old brother up and dressed before she goes to school. Besides she has to get herself ready for school and eat her breakfast. Sometimes she gets very irritated and feels she has too much to do. She fusses with the children and tries to hurry them and make them do more of the dressing themselves. The children tell their mother, and things get very unpleasant. What would you suggest doing about it? Here is a practical problem, one that· calls for thinking, for considering values, for weighing possibilities.

A practical home problem

There are plenty of schoolroom problems that need solving, problems in which the students are directly involved, that are practical and useful for homework. A third grade had to move to a new room. The teacher saw the necessity as an opportunity for some problem solving. The students were given problems to work on, involving measurements of the new quarters and of equipment to be moved; the counting of chairs; consideration of placement of furniture in light of the work of the group; plans for arrangement of supplies so that they would be convenient for use. They were practical problems involving use of both knowledge and skills. Details were discussed at school, but it was at home that the real thinking was done; and students soon came in with ideas, with drawings they had made to show furniture placement, and the like.

A practical
school
problem

PRACTICE OF SKILLS

This is one area in which children and young people really give themselves a workout. Go past an athletic field during after-school hours, and take note of the strenuous practice going on. One can almost feel the inner urge to develop more and more skills.

Drop by where baton twirling practice is in process. How they work! Listen to parents' tales of how impossible it is to get that girl away from her baton long enough to do any home chores.

Practice
is
natural

Go up and down any street, and notice the baseball practice under way, or notice children jumping with pogo sticks or playing marbles or jumping rope or turning somersaults. Wherever one finds children and young people one finds the practice of skills.

What have these activities to do with the practice

of school-learning skills? A great deal. They illustrate the willingness to practice until skill is gained
when there is the drive of interest. A teacher does
well to harness that willingness to homework that
has enough challenge to spark the interest drive.

It is easily understandable that interest tends to
drain off and willingness to practice ebbs when
the homework falls into "the same old stuff" class.
It takes imaginative planning to keep the drill and
practice type of homework alive, vital, and challenging, but it can be done. Whether the students
are in high school or grade school, practice in the
gaining of skills is essential, and their voluntary
leaning toward it in out-of-school activities is a useful starting point.

MEMORIZING

It is natural to leave much of the necessary memorization to homework assignments when the student
can, presumably and hopefully, settle down and
concentrate on doing it.

One had best be watchful, though, and plan that
the memorization is more than mere rote learning.
Otherwise one may find a student like the one
whose father tells about helping her with her assignment to memorize the preamble to the Constitution of the United States. They worked together
on it until she could repeat it letter perfect. Just as
they were about to sign off for the night, curiosity
prompted a question from her: "What is a preamble?" and then, "What is a constitution?"

Memorization is a legitimate type of homework, but it should be memorization with meaning. It can be so if thought is given to the planning of the assignment, whether the students be older or younger, and whether the subject matter be poems, beautiful prose, necessary facts, or rules for correct grammatical usage.

MAKING, DOING, CONSTRUCTING, CREATING

These are driving, impelling interests that little children bring to school in great measure. Sometimes they keep them as they go through grade school and into high school. Sometimes they lose them along the way.

"Oh, I know what we could do," one hears a little one say, and then out comes some new idea. They take sticks and stones and turn them to their play purposes. They take words and twist them into fantastic nonsense or use them to put some thought into poem or story form. They take pencil, paper, crayons, scissors and make objects of their own design.

Such activities, teamed up with homework, can produce amazing results as a student takes knowledge gained, procedures mastered, skills established and mixes them with his own individual initiative and imagination. Why should not homework free a student to use all the initiative he has? Why should it not provide an opportunity to put his knowledge and skill together in new and original ways? It is good sense to use creative drive in carrying school learnings on to new depths, to open up for the students a realization of the infinite possibilities that lie in their use.

Creative activities point to kinds of homework with built-in momentum; homework that takes students on and on into discoveries and search for knowledge; that opens the way for problem solving; that weaves multiple skills into a fabric of usefulness; that frees initiative and thought and offers encouragement in moving out of the stereotype and humdrum into the original and exciting.

Deciding which type of homework will accomplish the purpose at any particular time in any particular classroom is an essential part of any teacher's daily planning, whether it be for high school or elementary classes. Uppermost in mind must always be the question, What is it I want to accomplish? What is it I want the students to get from this assignment? Is it practice of some skill? Is it to stimulate independent thinking? Is it to encourage them to independent digging for facts? Is it to stimulate them to apply known facts in solving some problem? Is it to open the way for discovery of knowledge for themselves? Is it to open up some new idea to them? Is it to set them to thinking about some basic fundamental truths or values? Is it to give them opportunity for enjoyment of beautiful literature? Is it to strengthen their ability to observe with accuracy and awareness?

Relating type to purpose

Over and over a teacher must ponder questions such as these if homework is to be useful. There

remains, then, the choice of which kind of homework will best serve the purpose.

Variety Adds Spice to Homework

Just as variety is the spice of everything else, so is
it the spice of homework. Within each of the general
groupings mentioned lie endless possibilities and
variations.

There is no reason why homework should not be
interesting, challenging, sometimes exciting, out of
the humdrum, and into the stimulating. Not that all
of it can be so exciting that the student can hardly
wait to get home to start it. Inevitably there is
much homework that would not fall into that category, homework that nevertheless must be done.
Even so there *can* and, we maintain, *should* be such
variety that a student does not assume that just
because it is homework, it is going to be boring.

High school seniors, in order to produce the kinds
of English themes that befit seniors, must of necessity have had homework and more homework in
writing as they came along in the grades. Think it
over—the practice in forming the letters, in joining
them to form words, in putting them together to express ideas, in gathering ideas and information to
put into written form, in putting sentences together
so that ideas follow each other in logical sequence,
in constructing the theme so that paragraph sup-
ports paragraph with words so chosen that ideas
show forth with clarity and beauty—great amount

Variety
spices
needed
practice

of homework is necessary to achieve these skills as school year follows school year.

It is the same with oral English. In back of the high school senior's skill in selecting and preparing material for presentation and the poise in appearing before a group lie year upon year of learning. Homework is part of the means for bringing that learning into being. This holds true for all other subjects.

What infinite possibilities all those years hold for variety in the homework assignments. And how that variety can broaden and deepen outlook and understanding and bring skills to ever greater perfection.

Variety stimulates effort

There is no denying that it takes great thought to provide variety in homework which is challenging, stimulating, interesting, and impelling to effort. But —how much more satisfying to spend time planning such assignments than to spend it struggling with assignments that meet apathetic indifference or open rejection. Homework that is varied, by its very variation, puts individual abilities to work, catches individual interests, and offers opportunity for exercise of individual skills.

Often there can be not only variety in type but variety for individual students, variety geared to individual needs, fitting those who forge ahead of the others, those who take everything at a slow pace, those who have some special difficulty.

Sometimes, though not always, it is possible to plan work that allows student choice even while basically the same skill or procedure or application of fact is being emphasized. Thus a junior high teacher who wanted the students to gain greater skill in searching for reference material independently let them choose among ten different subjects on which they would do their research. All were directed to look for information in material available to them at home or in the public or school library or through interviews with persons experienced in the subject chosen. The basic purpose was the same for all, but the latitude allowed provided not only for individual interests but for varied home and neighborhood facilities.

It takes thoughtful planning to provide varied homework, just as it always takes thoughtful planning to do any good teaching.

Allowing
for
choice

Take Homework Beyond the Textbook

The textbook is a good place to start with homework but not a good place to stop. Through homework a teacher can open up to students broader views than the textbook provides. Through homework they can be guided to put what the textbook offers to work in practical ways; they can be stimulated to dig deeper than schooltime allows; and the way can be opened for going beyond their textbooks.

The textbook, and/or the curriculum material outlined, gives the starting point for the homework because it sets the learnings to be emphasized and the material to be covered in any specific school year. One does well to look upon them as guides, not as limitations. They do not preclude examining all the myriad details along the highway of learning; nor do they preclude students' thinking deeply as they travel along. Homework that takes them beyond the outlined curriculum material can make all that is learned from that material come alive. Homework can put that knowledge to work in everyday experience and can strengthen it through use.

Strengthen textbook learning

GO INTO EVERYDAY INTERESTS

One can go beyond the textbook into the students' everyday interests which offer the opportunity to use the wealth of assorted knowledge picked up outside of school.

A fourth-grade teacher, thinking of ways to tie homework to interests, set out to discover what these might be in that particular classroom. What was found? More than one might guess. One girl was collecting dolls and already had a sizable collection with many foreign ones included. Another was collecting miniatures, tiny dishes, tiny animals, anything tiny. A boy had aspirations to be a radio ham operator and was well on his way. Another had gone in for stamps. Another could tie just about every kind of knot but was looking for more. A girl already had two scrapbooks filled with pictures of cute babies but "none as cute as our own." Another reveled in drawing maps and kept the ones she thought were good in a special scrapbook. A boy always carried a magnifying glass in his pocket because he never knew when he might come upon

Individual interests are many

another bug to examine. One girl searched every magazine for pictures of ballet dancers. Another had a collection of records an adult might envy and knew them by name and composer. A boy planned to be a veterinarian and was always on the lookout for animals needing care. A girl aspired to being a jockey and knew the names of famous ones, both current and past. A boy was already handy with tools and delighted in the hours he could spend at the workbench. Another would rather be given the makings of boat models than anything he could think of. Another spent the hours that many spend with baseball in practice twirling a lasso. So it went in that one classroom. What a gold mine of knowledge and interest to utilize and to tie in with the homework! What a range of subjects for writing purposes! What a multitude of words for spelling! What a range for use of arithmetic facts and skills!

General as well as individual group interests point to possible paths beyond the textbook. A junior high teacher with ardent scouts in the group, both boys and girls, started them digging into the history of the Scouts. As they gathered material they were directed to compare the dates of this event or that to what was happening in both United States and world history at the same time; to figure out who was President of the United States at the given times; and who were the rulers in other countries that they happened to be studying. They went beyond the textbook to an outside interest and back into the textbook with some good solid homework well-done.

TIE HOMEWORK IN WITH FAMILY LIVING

Homework by its very nature goes into family living. There is plenty there to which to relate it.

A junior high social studies teacher in a city's low-income area, well aware of the problems of making money stretch, got together with the mathematics teacher. Together they figured out a series of assignments geared to the actual living conditions of the families in the area, assignments that made sense to the students because they dealt with conditions in which they were living and with which families had to cope daily.

Gearing homework to living conditions

A sixth-grade boy came to school with news that his father was going to build a garage, and he was going to help him. The teacher saw an opportunity. That garage became a class project. For homework the students measured it; discussed the material for it; and estimated its costs. They observed as bricks were laid, roof put on, concrete floor poured, shelves installed, inside painting done. It was visited frequently by the group and even more frequently by individual students. The teacher said, "I would never have believed so much good, solid homework could come out of one enterprise like that." With the exception of a few who were not especially interested, all the students worked as if it were their own. There will always be a few on the fringes less interested than the others. When another type of homework comes up, they may be among those in the midst of it.

A home activity may offer useful experience

Homework cannot always be tied to some particular project in some particular family, though often it can, and profitably so. When second-grade Richard's grandmother was flying from France to visit them, he was all agog over the time of the plane's takeoff and its arrival. The teacher told the children to ask at home about any air trips anyone in the family or friends of the family had taken and to gather any information they could from their parents about air travel. It was very simple homework, but it was a general tie-in with family living and was utilized for gathering information for school use.

Utilizing
home
events

With older children it could have been the step-off for exploring time changes, the crossing of the date line, the way time changes are arrived at, the changes involved in flying around the world, and perhaps examination of flight schedules, points of touchdown of different lines, the requirements of runways to accommodate jets, the speed of travel, and the like.

It makes homework practical when family-living types of activities are used as the vehicles for the learning one wants to emphasize.

RELATE HOMEWORK TO THE COMMUNITY

Similarly, homework comes alive when one takes it beyond the textbook into the community. It is one thing when seventh graders are given a chapter to study about city government setups and are told to make a chart showing two different types. It is quite another when, after a field trip to the local city hall for firsthand information, they are in-

First-
hand
information

structed to make a chart showing the setup they
heard about, with another chart showing a different setup, either one they have read about or one
their parents can tell them about, perhaps one from
some other place they have lived.

For several weeks an eighth-grade teacher tied in
homework with a community celebration of the
150th anniversary of the town's founding. It was a
relatively small community, and everyone was in-

Utilizing a
community
celebration

volved in preparations. The school, of course, had a
part. The eighth graders wanted to make one of the
floats for the parade, and as they thought of the
possibilities, their ideas grew and grew and the
teacher's grew with them. Such a variety of homework came out of it! The preparations were not
extraneous to schoolwork. They *were* schoolwork,
and every subject was involved. The teacher saw to
it that this was so. Homework played a part—homework that included history, arithmetic, writing of
reports, searching for information, and making
notes—everything.

Homework, thoughtfully planned, can take students beyond the textbook into a study of community industries and businesses, large and small,
different types of store buildings, of homes, and
public services, of recreational opportunities offered,

Studying
the
community

of the public library and police protection. It can
take them to the newspapers to discover events of
community significance, the manner in which
notices of intention for public improvements are
made known, tax notices, the action of the city
council, the activities of service clubs, the news

about the schools, notices of cultural events and reports on the same, and the setup, format, and presentation of all of these. It is the raw material out of which a teacher can assign homework that begins with the textbook but that goes beyond it further and further into the students' living experiences.

OTHER PEOPLE'S EXPERIENCES

There is the possibility, too, of going beyond the textbooks into other people's experiences. When the subject of pets or language or science has come up in reading, a teacher may ask the children to talk with their parents and find out from them which pets they had as children and which ones they enjoyed most, or if they didn't have pets of their own, which ones they knew about from friends. This is taking them into parents' experiences. It is broadening their knowledge by putting them in touch with the knowledge of others. It is giving them a wider vision of the feelings of others by letting them reach into their experiences.

Utilizing parent experiences

A teacher is taking students into the experiences of others when he directs them to the autobiographies or biographies of people who have done interesting, worthwhile things, when he asks them to read certain selected portions to try to figure out how the conditions under which those people lived were a factor in their actions. He takes them into the experiences of others when he asks them to look up and be ready to tell about the national holidays of different countries, or to think of all the different ways they have heard of people taking vacations, or

Touching many people's lives

to talk to someone in business about the different careers he considered before coming to his present occupation.

A high school sophomore said with wonder in her tone, "I never dreamed my mother wanted to be a concert pianist and almost was, and it makes me feel funny whenever I think about her taking care of all of us instead of doing it, but she says she would rather have us, and that makes me feel still funnier." Homework that leads students into deeper understanding has been well planned with an eye to its practical usefulness.

How Much? And When?

The amount and timing of homework is a potent factor in its usefulness and a salient point in its planning. There can be such an amount that it discourages any effort to get it done. The amount given needs to fit the ability to do it as neatly as the proverbial glove fits the hand that will wear it. Better a little that is done with satisfaction of accomplishment than much that is left undone with a feeling of guilt because of its unfinished state.

An overload is discouraging

Homework that overbalances the rest of living either within any one day or week stands the chance of being only half done, if done at all, and is often done in the face of energy-wasting resistance.

The amount pertains not only to that for one assignment but to the number of assignments within the week. It is as refreshing to have an occasional respite from homework as from dishwashing.

Giving homework in judicious amounts points to the necessity of the teacher's looking beyond the classroom in planning it. Students live under greatly varying conditions, some conducive to getting homework done, some definitely not. Some goes into homes where there is little or no interest in it, some where there is great interest. Some students have out-of-school jobs. Most have home duties. Many have outside activities. It is right that they should. They need time for recreation, time for a change of pace. They should have it. There are family activities into which they must fit the moment they come home from school. A teacher may not, usually does not, know what they are, but one can know full well they are there. Homework is important, but it is not all of living. It has a great usefulness, but so do other phases of living. A teacher must consider all of these factors in planning her assignments.

Other activities besides homework

When shall homework be given? Every day? Over the weekend? Over holidays? On certain days of the week and not on others? No one can lay down a flat and invariable rule that will work for all. A teacher must take into account differences from group to group. Variable conditions from day to day and week to week within any one year and with any one group must be considered. The only flat rule one could give would be to take students and conditions into account and plan accordingly.

Take conditions into account

It all points to the fact that homework, if it is to be useful, takes planning and more planning. It cannot be left to chance any more than any other phase of good teaching can. Like all good teaching it is fashioned out of thought and understanding of the students, the subject matter, and the resources at hand. These must be put together with planning that has sights set on purpose. Add to this the free play of imagination that never once lets it drop to the humdrum and stereotyped but keeps it alive and sparkling—not necessarily with excitement but always with the animation that keeps it moving—and one has homework that is an effective teaching tool.

4

Assigning the Homework

IT would be an interesting and probably a highly enlightening experience if teachers could follow some of their homework assignments into the homes where they are supposed to be done to see what happens. It might presumably give valuable hints on how and how not to give them.

There are definite and specific techniques for giving homework assignments, just as there are definite and specific guidelines for planning what to give. They are simple, easy, sensible techniques based on solid principles of learning and good teaching. Putting them into practice smooths the way for teacher and students alike.

It is the assignment that brings the homework the teacher has planned and the students together. It is an indispensable connecting link. Let that link be weak, and no matter how well the homework is planned its purpose is likely to remain unfulfilled or at best only partially fulfilled.

Visualize the Students Doing the Homework

Visualizing the students doing the homework is essentially an effort toward understanding. It gives a teacher the cue for the way to plan the assignment so that it will fit.

Often a teacher at first finds it difficult to do this visualizing. One may not foresee what the students' reactions will be, where difficulties will lie, where gaps in experience will make the assignment unintelligible. With this, as with all else, skill comes with experience. It comes more quickly, easily, surely, when the teacher makes a point of becoming acquainted with students individually, becoming acquainted with their parents, learning something of their homelife.

Get acquainted with students and homes

Sometimes there is a tendency to think of such acquaintanceship as being more pertinent to grade school students than to high school. Not so. The principle is the same. Reaction to homework is individual no matter what the grade level or age of the student. Only as a teacher can, in some measure, visualize the general trend of the reactions, can the homework be so planned and so assigned that it will make the connection one wishes it to make.

THINK OVER THE GROUP

An eighth-grade teacher working with students in language arts had as one broad objective to help them increase and broaden their vocabulary. At one point there appeared the need for both speaking and writing to be livened with a greater variety of descriptive words than most of the students had at their command. Homework was one means to accomplish the purpose. In planning the assignment the teacher thought to have them search through magazines and newspapers for words that would convey the idea of large, small, beautiful, happy, forceful, active, and on through a considerable list.

So much for planning. Now for thinking about the group with reference to the assignment. In mentally visualizing the group the teacher realized that there were some who would have neither magazine nor newspaper in the house. They could not fulfill the assignment, yet it would not be their fault.

Visualization of group affects planning

Then he thought of the possibility of their doing the assignment independently. Could they? Were most of them able to? How many would have parents who could or would help them? Would it serve the purpose to have parents help, or was this the kind of assignment where one of the purposes was to stimulate independent work?

The teacher decided that the first assignment, that of sending them to magazines and newspapers, would not work. So a change was made. A dittoed sheet was made for each student, giving a list of 100 words. The assignment then, it was decided, would be for them to search through this list and sort out the words that conveyed the idea of large, small, and so on.

The mental picture of the students doing the assignment helped the teacher make it one that they *could* do with some probability of success. This is one vitally important step before moving into the actual giving of an assignment.

THINK ABOUT THE INDIVIDUAL STUDENTS

Visualizing students doing the homework planned is essentially trying to imagine oneself in their homework situation. Which ones have an afterschool job? Which ones have responsibility for younger brothers and sisters because of a mother who works? Which ones have reference materials at home, and which do not? Which come from crowded homes where there is little if any place for quiet work? Which have parents who are interested in the homework to the point of trying to provide facilities for it, and which do not? A teacher cannot know every detail about every student, but what *is* known helps immeasurably in giving an assignment so that it appears to the student as something possible to do.

Individual differences a factor

Further, how are different students going to hear the directions one has in mind for doing the work? Which ones will remember them until they get home with enough clarity to follow them and translate them into action? Which ones are likely to have trouble with this or that part of the assignment? How can it be given so that the difficulty will not be an insurmountable hurdle?

In thinking over assignments with reference to individual students a teacher needs to be mindful of the fact that homework goes into many different types of homes. Not every home has a telephone. Nor do families in all homes sit down to their meals together. There are those whose eating is catch-as-catch-can. There are parents who neither read nor understand English. There are homes where no books, magazines, or newspapers can be found, where indeed there are none in the whole neighborhood. There are students who have no suitable place for doing homework, where there is not even suitable place for the family to sleep, homes where there is no plumbing, electricity, nor piped water.

All of this has a bearing not only on the planning of assignments but on the way assignments are given. Thinking over the assignment with reference to individual students means taking into account all factors that one can possibly know about.

Start the Students Thinking About the Assignment

Dropping students into a homework assignment without preparation has a very chilling effect. Starting them off on a line of thinking about the assignment serves to warm them up a little for it. It gets them set for doing it, gets the wheels of thinking about it moving.

BEGIN THINKING ABOUT IT IN THE CLASSROOM

Let's suppose that a third-year high school group is working with the general subject of the development of the United States as a nation and the specific topic of World War II. The teacher has tentatively planned a series of class discussions with correlative homework which, it is hoped, will strengthen the concepts developed in class. It is time for the first assignment. It makes good sense to work up to it, to open the door of thinking on it.

For high school young people World War II is history that is far removed in point of time from their experience. But there are probably persons closely related to the young people who are old enough to bridge the gap. So by way of preparation for launching into the assignment the teacher opens the way in class by asking different ones to tell what they may know about the war from experiences of their fathers, perhaps, or of relatives, or friends of the family. Thus one leads into the assignment.

Or take a third-grade teacher who is planning that the children write at home a simple account of "The Most Beautiful Thing I Have Seen in the Last Day." One *could* plunge them into it by telling them with no preliminaries what they are to do. But it would be poor judgment to do so. One would have only oneself to thank if no homework were done or if the little that did get on paper was stiff, stilted, and largely devoid of ideas.

No, if one expects homework to be done, one best get the thinking about it under way before the students are left with it. "The Most Beautiful Thing I Have Seen in the Last Day"—what an opportunity such a subject gives a teacher to help students become alert to beauty they may have passed unnoticed, to help them think discriminatively and selectively about what they did notice, to put their ideas into words that will convey their thought about it to others.

Relate to something known

"I saw something very beautiful on the way to school this morning," the teacher says to the group. "It was a drop of dew on the tip of a blade of grass." What happens? One child, then another, comes up with, "I saw something beautiful, too. It was—" and the subject for the homework that the teacher has in mind opens up wider and wider with each telling. (Incidentally some good practice in oral expression is going on.)

Present an idea as starter

"There are a great many things," the teacher says, "that sometimes we do not think about as being beautiful, though they really are." Then together they begin to think of some of these, such as a bridge with its graceful arches or a house with a beautiful door. That starts the children thinking of other types of beauty. Thus thinking is under way that makes the assignment natural and nothing to be feared. "Not just any beautiful thing," the teacher says, "but what seems to you the most beautiful."

No matter what the age of the students, high school juniors or seniors or third graders or second graders, the principle is the same—to get thinking under way so that the assignment has enough familiarity not to repel by its strangeness and to enable the students to go at it with confidence and not with fear.

A VARIETY OF WAYS TO GET
THINKING UNDER WAY

Sometimes getting thinking under way is accomplished by merely bringing up the subject and get-

ting general ideas about it stirred into activity.
Sometimes one does it by means of a picture or
question or account that focuses attention and
starts students thinking along some specific line.
Sometimes it is done by taking one student's experience as a stimulus to others to tell of similar experiences.

Get attention focused

This happened with an alert sixth-grade teacher.
One of the students arrived on a Monday morning
still excited about a weekend experience. The family had been on a trip some 150 miles away to visit
relatives. The trunk of their car had been broken
into and a considerable amount of clothing and
other articles taken. Through the quick work of the
police in the community where they were visiting
practically everything that had been taken was re-
covered.

The teacher took the children straight into a discussion of different ways in which people and property were protected in their own community. This
was something coming up soon in social studies,
and there was no need to wait. Here it was in a
practical, useful form. Nothing theoretical about it.
It was a practical incident alive with meaning. With
that as a starter and with thinking about it already
under way a homework assignment was given. The
children were asked to think over, notice, talk with
parents, and make a list of all the different ways
protection was being given to them, to their families, to their property right there in their own community.

Utilize current experience

This was a matter that did not need to be explored further in classroom discussion, since the teacher wanted the children to reach out and think independently on the basis of the thinking that was started by the discussion of the incident brought to the group.

In whatever way one may find to do it a homework assignment is going to be done more easily and more effectively if thinking is opened up before the assignment is undertaken, even though it may be only a little way.

Be Specific and Definite

There is no place in homework for vague, indefinite, obscure assignments. They only leave students hesitant, faltering, uncertain, doubtful how to begin, confused about what to do once they have begun, and puzzled as to whether they have accomplished what was expected when they finally do get something done.

Assignments should be definite, specific, and clear as to what is expected.

BE DETAILED ABOUT DIRECTIONS

One way of being definite is to give detailed directions instead of a general one such as "Read the next chapter, and be ready to discuss it." Discuss it from what point of view? Discuss it by raising questions about it? Or by picking out main points and presenting them? Discuss it from the standpoint

of agreement and reasons therefor or disagreement
and reasons for that? Be ready with points written
down or merely be ready with ideas in mind?

It is time well-spent from the last year in high
school right down through every grade to go into
detail about what is expected. It is this that fore-
stalls the time-wasting dawdling and dillydallying
that results because the student did not know what
the teacher wanted. Homework that is set up with
detailed directions stands a good deal better chance
of being done than when it leaves students wonder-
ing both what to do and how to do it.

**Define
expectations**

The argument is sometimes raised that when directions are too detailed, it leaves no room for individual initiative. There can be enough directions to
remove uncertainty and still leave plenty of opportunity for tackling an assignment in individual ways
—if it is that kind of assignment in the first place.
As a matter of fact clearing out uncertainty is a big
help in freeing thought so that whatever initiative
there is can come to the fore unhampered.

**Forestall
uncertainty**

This matter of giving assignments with enough
detail so that students know what to do is something to begin way down in the grades and something to keep at in every grade.

Some third graders came up with a beautifully
done bit of research which could never have come
out so well had the teacher not had an eye out for
detailed directions. The whole thing was informal
but not vague. They were planning some garden
planting when the matter of soaking seeds came up
because of one child's statement that his father

often soaked them. There was considerable investigation into the reasons for doing it. Then the teacher suggested a bit of homework—a little exploration into gathering information through first-hand experimentation and observation.

Nasturtium seeds and small seedling cups were provided for planting. Each child had two cups, one for soaked seeds, one for nonsoaked. Directions for the experiment were discussed, written on the chalkboard, and then put on dittoed sheets so each could have one to take home to follow. The directions read: (1) Put two seeds in one-fourth cup of water. (2) Let them soak four hours. (3) Make two holes one-half-inch deep in the cup marked S (they had marked the cups at school S for soaked, U for unsoaked). (4) Put one seed in each hole. (5) Cover with dirt. (6) Do the same with the unsoaked seeds in the cup marked U. (7) Sprinkle the dirt in each cup lightly with water each day. (8) Write down the date the first sprout appears, and tell whether it was in the S or the U cup.

Definiteness aids independence

Those students were able to carry on their experiment independently because of the sureness, exactness, and definiteness of the directions for doing it.

SET THE LIMITS WITHIN WHICH TO WORK

An assignment which is specific and definite sets limits within which to work instead of leaving a field so wide open that students do not know where to start nor where to stop.

A seventh-grade teacher had been working with the students on selecting words in their writing that

would convey definite facts and also the feeling of
the writer about the fact. A homework assignment
was to take the sentence "It is a winter day" as the
plain, simple fact to start with. The students were
told to keep that fact in mind but to rewrite the
sentence five times with such addition of words
that, while it would remain one sentence, it would
each time convey varied feelings of the person writing. In class they experimented with the sentence
to get a feeling for what was being asked. They suggested ways of rewriting the sentence that would
make one feel (1) like getting a heavier coat; (2)
glad he could be outside; (3) concerned lest there
was going to be a storm. The sentences were to con-
tain not more than twelve words each.

Such directions set limits and provided boundaries that prevented going off in tangents in all directions. They helped to hold the students to the
point and to direct their efforts to a specific end.
Here is some fine guidance toward good study
habits.

**Limits
prevent
diffused
effort**

ALLOW FOR INITIATIVE

The question arises whether being definite and
specific in giving directions and in setting limits
and boundaries is likely to be inimical to the use of
initiative. Does it deter the one who might forge
ahead and do more than what is assigned? No. It
need not.

If the teacher welcomes the use of initiative, there
is never any lack of opportunity to encourage it,
even though the assignments are laid right on the

line. Take the one for the seventh graders cited above. The lines were laid. The assignment as given showed what was expected. Beyond that, however, were possibilities of experimenting further with the idea, of writing more sentences to convey more different feelings, or of using another initial sentence and rewriting it to give different feelings.

Definiteness does not preclude initiative

A teacher can always point to possibilities beyond the assignment and encourage those who have the urge to go beyond it to do so. The very fact that the assignment is specific and definite gives the students who want to use some initiative a starting point from which to take off. One can be specific and definite without being binding and dogmatic.

Start Them with the Feeling of Know-how

It seems obvious that homework stands a much better chance of being done if students approach it with the feeling that they know how to go about it. This suggests clearly the wisdom of making sure that they start with a clear idea of how to work at whatever the assignment may be.

HELP THEM KNOW HOW TO ORGANIZE MATERIALS

One of the topics in an eighth-grade curriculum in science was "Water and Its Uses." In that particular state a large dam was in the process of being built. The teacher planned to tie this dam in with a study that would lead to wider understanding of the significance of legislation affecting the control of water usage; the effect on the lives of people of building dams to supply water for large areas; the changes made in the productivity of those areas with the availability of water; the necessity for flood control; and so on.

One particular homework assignment which illustrates the point of helping students organize materials had to do with water as it affected their lives and their homes. The class had first approached the subject through class discussions. The first assignment was merely to notice and write down each use they saw being made of water.

Step by step

The lists that came in were general, as the teacher had known they would be. That led to the next step which was to sort out the different items and group them in some form of logical relationship. They talked about how the grouping might be uses of water in homes, neighborhood, community. Or it might be uses of water for homes, for business, for recreation. Each one was to decide on his own general groupings, then fit all the items on his list into those groupings. No need to go into the assignments that followed, nor the use to be made of this one. The point here is that the students were being helped to see how to organize ideas.

Specific suggestions on organization

"Make a list of this or that," a teacher often says, in connection with some piece of homework. But how does one make lists that are more than a heterogeneous conglomeration of items? That was what the teacher in the previous illustration was doing. She was helping them organize their materials.

"Now think over what you will need to do this

assignment," another teacher says. The students are being helped to organize their materials for the purpose at hand.

"Remember," says another, "when you write to select your main points and then think of the details you will bring in to support those points." Thereby the students are being reminded of how to organize their writing in a way to present it forcefully. It is a matter of helping them go about the homework in an orderly way instead of a hit-or-miss haphazard way.

HELPING THEM USE RESOURCE MATERIAL EFFECTIVELY

Skill in using resource material is a matter of continuous learning that should begin in the grades and progress with each school year. Homework assignments can contribute significantly in strengthening that skill and broadening the knowledge of materials to be used.

Let's say a ninth-grade group is involved with the study of public speaking. Each one is to prepare a five-minute talk on a subject of his own choosing, the talks to be given to the group at intervals during a two-week period. The preparation is homework. Assume that the subjects have been decided upon after ample discussion on the selection of an interesting topic and a review of some of the fundamental principles of public speaking.

The purpose here is to help the students use resource material effectively. One can assume that

Preview possible resources

they have had practice using resources in previous school years, but one can also assume that they have not yet gained the ultimate skill in doing so. Here is the opportunity to talk with them about the different kinds of resources available, encyclopedias, (at home if they have them, at the public library, or in the school library), perhaps their own textbooks if any of the subjects chosen are covered there, magazines and newspapers, their own parents, other adults they may know, perhaps their own observations, maybe their own experiences or observations—all depending on what the subject is. Often students do not realize what resources they can turn to. Frequently it doesn't occur to them that other people are valuable as resources for information, opinions, experiences.

Taking notes

Once the resources are located and consulted, however, what shall they do with the information they come upon? How can they gather it together so that they can make use of it? The organization spoken of in the previous section comes into play here. Skill is needed in taking notes. What shall one put down? How full should notes be? All of this is part of using resource material. Bringing out the types and locations of resource materials is part of helping students make use of them, but clarifying the way to use resources for their purposes is likewise essential.

KNOWING HOW TO MEMORIZE

It may be that the homework the teacher has planned calls for memorization, perhaps of a poem or some paragraph of prose that for some reason it seems wise for the students to know verbatim. It is one thing to give them the bare assignment to memorize something. It is another to help them know how to do it. It is wise first to go through the whole selection to get the feeling of it. Then go through to pick out the main ideas and get a mental picture of them in their consecutive order. Then notice the unusual, colorful, descriptive words associated with those ideas, and read it over as a whole, thinking about the ideas. Read again, and yet again, then look away from the written or printed lines, and think the first idea, the next, and so on.

Outline the steps

When students learn to memorize in such a way, they are doing more than merely memorizing words. They are memorizing ideas. They are doing what a sixth-grade child called "memorizing with our thinking," which the teacher had pointed out was the way to memorize.

Memorizing ideas

This emphasis on the know-how of memorization is as pertinent for the high school teacher as for the grade school teacher. Skills fall into disuse very easily unless there is constant refurbishing and continuous use.

Students, whatever the grade, can learn to memorize dates with their thinking when it seems necessary to store away some special ones. They can be helped to associate the given dates with events that give meaning to them, and to sort out the events and the dates in consecutive order. Then they will not be like the fifth-grade child whose grandfather

Associate dates with meaning

had asked him what dates he had learned in history, and he replied, "I know 1775 and 1492 and 1914 and 19— because that's when I was born, but I don't know what the others are about for sure except one of them is when Columbus got here by mistake."

When memorizing is given as homework assignment, the know-how of doing it calls for due attention. It is part of building up good study habits. It is putting a tool into the hands of students which can be useful to them long after the homework assignments are over and done.

LEARNING TO ORGANIZE WORK MATERIALS AND TIME

Another point for which help is needed in knowing how to do the homework is in gathering together materials to do it. Think of the time wasted as a student sits down to work, then has to go hunt for a pencil. Then the pencil is not sharp and must be sharpened. On the way to find something with which to sharpen it something else attracts attention. Finally, with prodding, he gets back to the place where he is supposed to be working. Then it is paper that is missing, or a ruler, or a different kind of pencil from the one he had sharpened, or some scotch tape, or an eraser because the one on the end of the pencil is too dirty to use, or he finds he has brought home the wrong book so he can't do the work after all.

It all goes back to thinking through what is needed, gathering it together, then going about the work. But, one asks, how can a teacher insure that materials for work will be gathered together in orderly fashion at home? One cannot *insure* it. One *can*, however, make it much more probable than otherwise by taking time when giving the homework assignment to raise the question of the materials that will be needed to do it and mentioning occasionally that precious time is saved by working in an orderly way.

How to work in an orderly way

Speaking of time—this is another point where students need help in knowing how to do their homework, in knowing how to plan their time so that they can get it done, in knowing how to divide the time they have so that each subject gets its share. Homework is a vehicle for teaching many things aside from the specific subject matter of the curriculum. When several teachers are giving homework, it makes good sense for them to get together on the amounts given so that it is possible for the students to accomplish it in the time available.

Budgeting time

Do Some of the Homework Yourself

Many a homework assignment would be shortened or revamped altogether if the teacher giving it sat down and actually did some of it. Often one would find that it is not so easy as it sounds, or that it takes longer to do than one had thought, or that there are sticky spots in it that one did not realize, or that some parts of it are just not within the students' ability.

PREVENTS ITS BEING TOO DIFFICULT

A high school student with an English assignment in front of him fretted and fumed and griped to anyone who would listen. He said that it was a "dumb" assignment, and that he didn't know how "she" could expect anyone to do it, and that there was too much of it in the first place.

The students had been working on different forms of writing. At the moment they were practicing different types of newspaper writing. The homework assignment, which covered a week's time including a weekend, was to write up at least five news items, a feature story of not more than 200 words, and an editorial opinion on some school, local, or national issue of interest, showing by the way the writing was done the differences in these types of writing. It was quite an assignment when one considered the fact that the students were getting their first experience in differentiating among these forms of writing and that they had homework in other classes as well as in English.

Consider inexperience

Chances are if the teacher had sat down to try out the assignment, she would have revamped it so that it would seem to the students more possible of completion. Gathering five news items and writing up each with an arresting lead sentence might have, at first thought, seemed simple against a background of experience. But students have not had experience. They have to decide what is news in the first place. They have to remember that it must have the what, why, where, when, how details, and they

Visualize the difficulties

must make note of these. They must remember the necessity for a lead sentence that attracts the reader, and more than that they must compose it. Then having done one item, there are four more to do, and that is only the beginning. Even granted that they had been practicing on each of the different types and that the teacher expected only amateurish writing, it is pretty likely that if she had sampled the assignment, it might have been modified.

KEEPS IT REASONABLE IN AMOUNT

Doing a sample of the work helps in keeping it down to an amount that it is reasonable to think can be done in the time available. A teacher should be very realistic about this matter of time. A student goes home from school with homework in the offing. He drops his books, heads for the refrigerator for a snack, turns on the TV. Time slips by. There are home chores to do, perhaps a paper route, maybe a part-time job. First thing one knows it is suppertime. Time for another favorite TV program. This is the way living is.

Must fit into other things

With this in mind let a teacher sit down and time the homework proposed, taking into account that the students are not going to do it as fast as a teacher can, that they will use some time getting down to work, that there may be a telephone call from or to a friend—and more time has slipped away. Besides, the students have to take in new ideas as they work, put skills into use that are not yet wholly perfected, work out procedures that do

Realistic timing

not yet come easily to hand, apply principles with which they are only now becoming familiar.

Gearing a homework assignment to a realistic appraisal of time required for doing it enhances the probability of its being done.

REVEALS DIFFICULTIES

Doing some of the homework one has in mind as a sample has a way of revealing spots where more explanation is needed than one had first thought, and sometimes shows up the whole assignment as being pretty unreasonable, though at first it had seemed a good idea.

It is probable that a tenth-grade biology teacher, had he sampled one assignment he gave, would never have given it, thereby saving the ire that was raised on the part of both students and parents. Harder than one thought The assignment was to get a skeleton and reconstruct it. Sounds simple, doesn't it? At least until one tries it out. Then the difficulties begin to come to light, difficulties recounted by the parents of one student who tried valiantly to complete the assignment. He finally did with the weekend help of the family. At a loss where to get a skeleton Mother came to the rescue with a chicken. It was cooked, the meat taken off the bones, the bones separated. Then came the reconstruction. After two hours of struggle with glue, scotch tape, adhesive, and rubber cement, it looked hopeless. Dad came to the rescue. Finally after hours of work, it was put together, although it was a shaky skeleton. Then it had to be painted.

It is a good idea for homework assignments to lie within the range of reasonable possibilities of accomplishment, and the teacher's trying them out is an eminently useful way of bringing difficulties to light.

This method enlightened a third-grade teacher who wanted the students to do some critical observing and thinking about comparative weight and size and incidentally to get some practice in writing and spelling. She jotted down some notes, thinking she would ask them to look around at home and write down things they saw that are (1) heavier than a book; (2) lighter than a pail of water; (3) bigger than a chair; (4) smaller than a pencil. Then realizing how unreasonably long the list would be, it was modified to five things under each heading. This was something the children could do. They enjoyed doing it. The combined lists written on the chalkboard brought both discussion and chuckles.

Suggests more reasonable limits

Often the result of doing some of the work oneself to get the feel of it results in more clearly defined directions. Sometimes it results in delaying the assignment until there have been more classroom experiences that will make it meaningful. Sometimes it eliminates the homework altogether and puts something simpler in its place.

May change the assignment

MAY SUGGEST PUTTING IT INTO WRITING

Sometimes after trying out the assignment, one realizes that the directions are going to put quite a responsibility for accurate recall on the students. Often it is wise to put homework assignments into writing—on a dittoed sheet that students can take with them for reference. It is a simple way to reduce the time-consuming and anxiety-laden bewilderment about what is expected. One knows what was meant because it is written down. Parents know, too.

Doing some of the work oneself is just one more means of making sure it fits the students who have to do it.

Get the Students to Work with You

Great energy is saved when teacher and students pull together on homework instead of the teacher pulling this way to get it done and the students pulling that way to keep from doing it! If all the student time spent on griping about homework was put into doing it, both homework and dispositions would benefit. When a teacher finds a way to clear away the obstructions to a cheerful and willing acceptance of homework, the learning possibilities for students are augmented significantly, to say nothing of the comfort added to both schoolroom and family living and the energy released for constructive effort. It can be done. It has been done. All of the suggestions already given point to some of the ways of doing it. There are others.

LET THE STUDENTS KNOW THE PURPOSE

Students know that they need practice in this skill and that. Why not let them know that this particular assignment is designed for that purpose? Why not say right out to them, "It is useful to know how to use a great many different words, and I am asking you to do this assignment to help you become acquainted with words you do not know now." Why not say forthrightly, "I could tell you the answers, but I want you to do some discovering for yourselves, so I am giving you this assignment." Why not tell them, "It is very useful to have these facts on tap, so I am asking you to memorize them."

Speak up forthrightly

Students are quick to understand what one is getting at if they are given the chance. It gives an impetus to their work when they accept the teacher's purpose as their purpose and go to work at it. It gives dignity to homework to know the purpose toward which it is directed. It gives confidence in the teacher who has a purpose that can be put into words. It gives students respect for themselves to know that they are considered capable of understanding the purpose for which the work is intended. There is always the possibility, too, of giving them the opportunity to offer ideas on the kind of homework that would be helpful to them in their learning. Students are pretty perceptive about their own needs.

They can get the point

BE READY TO GIVE HELP

It seems redundant to say that one of the ways to get students working with one on their homework is to work *with* them on it. A teacher can do so by offering to be in the classroom a half hour before school begins to help anyone who has had trouble either with the homework of the night before or of some due at a later date.

A teacher works with the students when he lets them know his willingness to stay after school to give similar help. A high school teacher gave the students his home telephone number and told them if they ran into snags to feel free to call him. He said not one of those students abused the privilege and that he felt it had given them complete assurance of the sincerity of his great desire to be of any help to them he could.

The very effort to make every assignment understandable, the willingness to explain again and again and never with impatience, lets the students know that one is working with them. It is in itself an invitation to give willing effort on their part. The effort to tie the homework to their experiences, to utilize the knowledge they have of things outside of school, is a way of working along with them. It gives them an open invitation to put all they have into doing the homework with a full measure of effort instead of resisting and resenting it.

One can assign homework in a way that gives the students confidence in their ability to do it, that sends them to it with assurance. One can assign it in a way that invites effort, that appeals to pride in doing it well, that stimulates satisfaction in work done honestly and through independent effort. One can give assignments in a way that turns students' thought to what they are learning instead of centering it on doing what is asked for the mere purpose of getting it done. In short, one can teach through the very way a homework assignment is given.

Willingness to help invites effort

Just good teaching

5

Examining and Using
the Homework

HOMEWORK, once it has been done, must be
examined and used in some manner if it is to achieve
its potential as a teaching aid and a means of furthering student learning. When it is so considered,
it becomes natural to examine and use it.

The term "examine" is used designedly in preference to the more usual terms "evaluating" or
"correcting." Examine is taken here to indicate a
going over of the work done, not so much to judge
its worth or to correct mistakes as to get an overall
picture of what the work shows of the student's
understanding and the state of his learning. Thus
it denotes a broader consideration than either
evaluation or correction, though both may be included.

Students Should Feel Assured It Will Be Examined

Whether the homework is a written essay, problems to be solved, a project to be worked out, ob-

servations to be made, information to be gathered, or whatever else, the students should know with no reason to doubt that the teacher will look at what they have written, listen to accounts of what they have done, give attention to the solution of the problems assigned.

NOT AS A GOAD, BUT AS AN INCENTIVE

The statement that homework should be examined should not be taken as any suggestion that such examination should be thought of or used as a goad to accomplishment, nor as a threat designed to keep the students at it. Rather it should be understood that the work is looked upon as important enough to merit examination. If there is added to this an assurance of interest in how it was done and the nature of the results produced, it serves as a wholesome incentive to work.

IT IS ONLY FAIR

It is only common fairness to take cognizance of what has been done once an assignment has been made. This is something students feel strongly about. A high school senior tells how a group of them hit upon a scheme to discover the correctness of their suspicion that their homework was not examined. Each agreed that here and there in their English assignments they would leave sentences unfinished or would introduce extraneous material. They did. Nothing happened. The boy said as he told about it, "We call it cheating on us, and you don't have much respect for a teacher that cheats like that."

RESPECT BEGETS RESPECT

Presumably one wishes students to respect their homework to the point of putting honest effort into it. The teacher then must accord it respect. Leaving it unexamined is not respecting it.

A fifth-grade class was given an assignment of forty-five problems in long division with instructions to prove their results. The papers were not collected. The next day they were again given forty-five problems with the same instructions.

These papers were not collected. The third day the assignment was repeated. By this time about half of the class had decided either through consultation with one another or individually that for them this was the end. They would not do the work.

"What's the use?" they asked one another, "She doesn't know whether we do them or not." This time, however, the papers *were* collected causing both consternation and worry. Some who had done the work jibed self-righteously, "Good enough for you." Then the worry eased. Word circulated through the grapevine that the papers had been seen in the wastebasket with no marks on them. The conclusion was that even though they were collected, they were not examined. Comments were plentiful and unfavorable. Respect begets respect and contrariwise.

The students know

TAKES IT OUT OF BUSYWORK CATEGORY

If homework is not to be dubbed busywork by the students, it must be examined. Both lack of examination or only routine check throws it into that category so far as the students are concerned. Whatever purpose the teacher may have in mind is lost to view once they get the idea that it is a time filler, "just something to keep us busy."

Even so, one may point out, it is in the students' interests to do the work, since presumably it provides experience in something in which experience is needed. True, but holding oneself to a task when the teacher gives no evidence of knowing whether it was done or how it was done calls for self-discipline that even high school students are unlikely to have achieved. Teacher attention to the work done is a commonly needed impetus to effort regardless of the ages of the students.

Whatever the teacher's purpose in giving the homework, if it is not examined it almost certainly gets labeled busywork and is bypassed altogether or given only token attention.

ADDS DIGNITY

Homework that is examined takes on a greater dignity than that which comes to an ignominious end in the wastebasket without so much as a glance cast upon it. It reaches a higher plane in the students' eyes when there is the assurance that the one giving it cares *how* it is done enough to scrutinize it. It adds even more prestige to it when the examination extends to consideration of the understanding and growth that it evidences. Whether or not there is any driving interest in doing the homework, it is reasonable to assume that some inner feeling of warmth is engendered when it is known that the teacher cares enough about it to spend time and energy looking at it.

The Time Factor

There is no denying the fact that it takes time to examine homework. Teachers often say that important as they know it is for them to do it, they do not have the time to do so properly.

CONSIDER TIME FACTOR WHEN PLANNING

Time is something to think about when planning the homework. It is better to assign an amount that *can* be examined than to pile on so much that it cannot. There is no surer way for students to develop poor study habits, irresponsible attitudes, or habits of pushing it aside as not worth the bother.

Not only is it wise to consider the amount of homework given but also to take into account the type given with an eye cast to the moment of reckoning when the homework has been done and is awaiting the teacher's thoughtful scrutiny.

IMMEDIACY IS IMPORTANT

The sooner that attention can be given to the examination of homework after it is done the better.

Students live in the immediate present. When they hand in work, they want to know at once how they did on it. It is uppermost in their minds.

"See how I fixed this," says a seventh grader. "Look, I put it down this way," says another. "I'll bet you don't know what I did on this page," from still another eager for comment.

A day goes by, and other interests press in on them. Details that were all important yesterday become vague. Interest lessens as attention turns to other matters that now hold the place of importance because of their immediacy.

As the thought of what was done slips into vagueness, so does its potential usefulness as teaching material. Time between the doing and the examining is of the essence.

SOME ASSIGNMENTS EASIER TO EXAMINE THAN OTHERS

When planning is done with the assumption that the homework will be examined, it makes sense to think ahead as to how that examination will be carried out and the time it will take, and to plan something that will not be so time-consuming as to be prohibitive at worst or discouraging at best. Some assignments are far more easily examined as a list than in essay form. The intent to provide practice writing in correct essay form suggests giving the assignment when there will be time to read the essays. It may be wise either to skip a day with no assignment or to give something to extend over

Consider examination when planning

several days, thus providing a cushion of time for going through the essays.

When the assignment is of the type that calls for exact answers, such as arithmetic problems or spelling words, one can make a list of the answers at the time of planning. With this at hand it is easy to quickly check through the work—not for correctness of answer *alone,* though. A teacher always needs pad and pencil nearby to jot down where this student had trouble or where that one obviously didn't understand the assignment or where another evidences need of additional drill on some item.

Note expected answers when planning

Teachers frequently find that they can examine the homework with less pressure and more thoughtfulness if they alternate days for assignments in different subjects, *e.g.,* something for language one day, arithmetic another, and so on. There is the added advantage of variation for the students.

Budget assignments

CAN SOMETIMES BE EXAMINED AS GROUP WORK

Sometimes assignments can be of a kind that lend themselves to examination as regular group work. A seventh-grade teacher, who had been working with the students on picking out the main idea of a paragraph, gave an assignment of this type, indicating given paragraphs in the social studies text, a different one for each student. They were to study the paragraph, pick out the main point, and be ready to present it to the group two days later.

One might say that it would be a tedious process for a group of thirty each to present the main idea of a given paragraph. It would have been if the teacher had had each do it in turn. But it was not

Give the students a part done that way. The class was divided into groups of five with each student presenting his work to the group. The teacher moved from group to group, listening as the students took their turns within their groups. At the time of planning the assignment, note was made of the main points of each of the paragraphs assigned, marked with the initials of the student to whom it was given. There they were at hand for quick reference during the class period. It was examination of homework and class participation and practice in identifying main points all rolled into one, besides gathering the information that the main points conveyed.

Examining homework need not be prohibitively time-consuming, and it need not be drudgery. It

Need not be drudgery should be neither the one nor the other. The secret of keeping it from being either lies, as has been suggested, in planning and assigning, in seeing it as part of the preparation for teaching, in using it as teaching material that comes live from the children, teaching material that stems from the textbook but goes beyond it into the children's living outside of school, teaching material that comes out of that living and supplements the text.

Use for Teaching Purposes

When homework is thought of, not as extraneous to teaching, but as an inherent part thereof, it blends into all of the teacher's preparation, planning, and actual classroom procedure.

PROVIDES DISCUSSION MATERIAL

An eighth-grade teacher desirous of alerting the students to environmental and social changes calling for human adjustments decided to use homework as a springboard to class discussions.

The subject was opened up with some questions in class about changes they may have noted due to a recent snowfall. Mention was made of a newly enacted local ordinance banning any parking on the streets between midnight and 7 A.M. After some discussion the assignment was given to bring in a list of all the changes of any sort noted during a period of one week.

Can be a spring-board

"Can it be changes that people have something to do with?" asked one student, "and not just changes like rain and those things?"

"Yes," the teacher said, "any kind of change." Off and on during the week one student and another would chuckle and say, "I found some funny changes, but I'm not telling."

When the day came that the lists were to be handed in, the students were eager to discuss them. It was an assignment that had caught their interest. "Can't we tell some of the things now?" one student asked. And another, "Yes, let's do it, because some of mine are funny."

What a letdown it would have been not to have given them the chance right then. The teacher did.

It was a lively, spontaneous exchange of a few items. The teacher had no intention of exhausting the discussion that was potential in the lists, so after a few good laughs, the work was put aside with the promise, "I'll enjoy reading all your lists, and we'll discuss them later."

When that discussion time came, there was material for more than one class period. There was mention of evaporation, as one would expect, and

Multiple possibilities

of freezing and of burning wood to produce heat. But observation had gone far afield from such as these. There were items such as, "I gained half a pound"; and "The baby cut a tooth"; and "Mother had her hair cut." There were items of blue jeans torn; of cream that curdled in the coffee; of kittens that opened their eyes; of a dish that broke and will never be a dish again; of an auto tire that blew out; of trash that was burned. The students mentioned nails pounded into a board; mothers who baked potatoes, and the potatoes would never be the same; paper that was changed by the holes punched in it; and household arrangements necessary to make room for a visiting grandmother.

What a wealth of material those papers provided, and how much would have been lost had the teacher not examined them minutely! What insight they gave to the students' thinking; what deeper understanding they brought of things they were alert to; what glimpses they gave of originality and initiative, where perhaps it had not been too evident before.

OFFERS STIMULUS TO USE OF INITIATIVE

A fourth-grade teacher with an eye on the curriculum outline for language arts gave a homework assignment designed to help the students feel free in their composition writing, free to let imagination roam, free to use ideas in new and original ways.

An opening sentence was given for a story they were to write at home. The sentence was, "A brother and sister were out walking when they met an elephant who said, 'Good morning, how are you today?'" There had been discussion of "just suppose" stories as contrasted with factual ones. They knew this would be one of the former. It was not to be more than five sentences in length when completed. It was a two-day assignment since one of the students had said, "Don't you think we better have one night to think and one night to write?"

Initiative was wanted

Reading the papers and planning how to use them went along simultaneously, with the plan finally evolving to select at random papers to read at class time to the group. Another time the teacher might have made the selection, but in this instance it was felt any paper had something to offer that would be useful to the group.

Planning the use

The first one finished with, "The children were surprised. The children did not say anything. The elephant said, 'You are not very polite,' and walked away." That brought out the comment that he was right and that they were *not* very polite.

The next had a very different ending. It was,

Variety
opens
discussion

"They were so scared that they ran home fast. They told their mother. She would not believe that they saw an elephant." More conversation ensued about how different mothers would have responded.

Then came an ending, "The children said, 'Good morning, how about giving us a ride?' He did. They had a wonderful time."

As the reading went on there was discussion about the varied endings, how some of them were fanciful, how some students had used facts in unusual ways, how some had put together ideas from stories they knew, how it makes a story interesting to have conversation in it.

The teacher used the assignment to stimulate originality, then to bring out spontaneous discussion, then to point up details of writing in an interesting way, and in the next day's follow-up to bring out points about necessary spelling, capitalization, and punctuation before the stories would find their way into "My Storybook," which each one was compiling.

ESTABLISHES A STANDARD OF WORK

It was a standard of work that the teacher was establishing through the discussion of the endings and through the necessary corrections in the mechanics of writing the story down.

A standard can be established in many ways; for example, an English teacher in high school told her class, "This plot was built as a story plot should be because it—" and then went on to point out details needing emphasis.

A science teacher who had given the students a project to work on pointed out in a follow-up, "The important thing was that you took the problem, thought how it might be worked out, planned the steps for doing it, tried out what you had planned, thought where it might be bettered, revised your plan, and tried it out again." This teacher was defining for them the steps in going about their work in an organized, scientific way. Perhaps they worked that way, perhaps they didn't. For the ones who did, it was reemphasizing the way to work. For the ones who did not it was bringing it again to their attention. For all it was a follow-up that pointed out how homework in that particular area should be done. It was giving them a standard for work instead of leaving them to work it out as best they might.

Use to establish standards

Every piece of homework offers the opportunity for developing a standard, for clinching facts, bringing procedure into focus, and turning attention to results as related to the purpose to be accomplished.

SHOWS WHERE HELP IS NEEDED

To a discerning teacher each piece of homework has diagnostic value, revealing points where individual students are sure of their facts and procedures and where some point needs clarification, some skill needs strengthening, some closed door of thinking needs opening. To a teacher concerned with building individual strengths this kind of insight is invaluable.

A high school junior tells how in one class the instructor writes a note in the margin of a homework assignment that leaves something to be desired, saying, "If you will drop in, I'll help with this." It is understood with the students that he will be in his office before hours in the morning, after hours in the afternoon, and by appointment at other times to give help where help is needed. The young man telling the story comments, "It makes sense to do homework when something comes out of it that helps you." It does indeed.

It is the same whether it is a high school senior or a lower elementary school child or anyone between. When gaps in homework accomplishment mean indication of help needed and that help is forthcoming, it tends to take fear and an "I don't care" attitude out of homework and put purposefulness into it. A fifth-grade student summed it up succinctly in her comment, "I don't like homework because I'd rather look at TV, but you've got to have it because that's how the teacher knows where she's got to help you, and when she helps you that way it makes you get better grades."

AS LEADING-ON POSSIBILITIES

To an alert, discerning teacher homework often offers glimpses of interests that lead far beyond the immediate assignment. It sometimes reveals touches of originality and initiative that, nourished and tended, can open up whole vistas of accomplishment. It can suggest areas of exploration the teacher may not have thought of but that tie in with curriculum

Ready to help

Encourages purposefulness

Reveals originality

requirements in a way that will enrich and extend them in a way the teacher may not have foreseen.

A simple assignment given an eighth-grade group led on over a period of weeks in a way the teacher could not have foreseen, and but for his alertness might have ended in being merely another assignment. The students were asked each to write an account of his or her hobby. In case of no special hobby the account was to be of something of special interest. The class discussion that followed the examination of the papers brought out hobbies and interests that the students had no idea their classmates were following. The teacher said that it led to a closer acquaintance among them and an added respect. It led to discussion of hobbies of people they knew outside the classroom. It led to collecting items about the hobbies of people mentioned in the news; to investigating the hobbies of personages in history, literature, and science, as spoken of in their texts; to becoming interested in incidents of hobbies that had been known to lead into careers.

More than "another" assignment

Not all assignments would have the leading-on possibilities that this one held, and this one might not have had, either, in the hands of a less imaginative and alert teacher.

In a third grade where many of the children were very shy and inclined to be uncommunicative, the teacher had been utilizing every possibility to bring about a greater feeling of ease. One day they were told that a friend who was coming the next day to visit was very fond of cats. They were asked to think

An alert teacher

about any interesting things they knew about any cat which they could tell her, and maybe if they wanted her to, she would tell them about her own three cats.

It was a very simple assignment, and some might not call it homework, but it was schoolwork carried

over into home hours. It was a lively conversation period that the children and the visitor had together. There was plenty of opportunity for them to listen and to talk. The next day they were still full of tales they had to tell. But besides mere storytelling there was discussion of how, when many people have something to say, one has to think ahead and get ideas into a few sentences instead of rambling on and on. They talked about the many different kinds of cats they had heard about that day. Someone suggested that they bring in pictures of cats doing interesting things. They became discrim-

inating in what they considered a sufficiently interesting picture to merit a place on the bulletin board or in their "All About Cats" book which they thought they might write. As one child summed it up, "It's got to be something that isn't just a cat not doing anything unless it is a very unusually beautiful cat." Before the "All About Cats" book was finished, it contained clippings the children had found in newspapers or magazines about feeding cats, about their care, or feature stories of cat escapades or travels.

Many a homework assignment has just such leading-on possibilities. But, someone may ask, are not these illustrations merely examples of good teaching? Yes, they are. Giving useful homework and making use of what is done is part of good teaching.

The Students Should Know Where They Stand

It is still not enough to plan the homework wisely, to assign it thoughtfully, to examine it conscientiously, to follow it up in such a way as to make it useful for learning. The students should know where they stand on what they have done. Each one should know what he has accomplished, how proficiently he has accomplished it, how successfully he has achieved the purpose of the assignment.

It is his right to know. It is his work. He has put his effort into it, or has not, as the case may be. It is he that is supposed to be learning from it. He should know where he stands on it.

A TWOFOLD APPRAISAL

A twofold appraisal of homework is useful—the teacher's and the student's. The teacher's appraisal gives the student the point of view of one with more experience and broader knowledge; of one whose purpose is to help him with his learning; who sees as he cannot see the overall learnings of which this piece of work is a part; of one who looks ahead as he cannot to see where it fits into the whole; who can see where it may lead; who presumably is concerned not only with the learning

Teacher appraisal

involved in the subject matter but with what the whole experience is doing to the student as a person.

Student appraisal The appraisal of the student is a matter of helping him look with insight on what he has done; assess his accomplishment; and use his judgment of his achievement in relation to the standards set.

HELP STUDENTS TO KNOW HOW TO APPRAISE THEIR WORK

Students know better than anyone else the degree of effort they have put into their homework. This is one step in appraising it. However, important **Details of appraisal** as effort is, an accurate appraisal also includes assessment as to whether the homework is well-done, where it falls short, where it can be improved, the extent to which it has accomplished its purpose. This type of appraisal is a skill which even high school students must have help in learning. The sooner the know-how of such appraisal is made a part of the student's learning, the more readily he is likely to make it part of his way of work as he moves on from grade to grade.

A teacher who would help students establish this habit of self-appraisal and gain skill in doing it must be watchful to be clear, specific, definitive in his own appraisal.

Define terms "Good," a teacher writes on a fourth-grade spelling paper in which twelve out of fifteen words were spelled correctly. Does the "Good" refer only to the number of words correctly spelled or also to the legibility with which they were written? Was the orderly spacing on the paper considered as a factor? Was the capitalization of the necessary words taken into account? Answers to all of these questions are essential to knowing what the "Good" written on the paper means. Defining the term is part of helping a student learn to make accurate appraisal.

"Well-done," was written at the end of a paper turned in by a high school senior on conservation of natural resources in relation to the national economy. It was an assignment given after a series of readings and class discussions on the various aspects of conservation in which the instructor had endeavored to stimulate the students' interest and thinking. But what did the "Well-done" on the paper mean? Did it refer to information, to original thinking, to breadth of concept, to the manner of presenting the subject? These are details essential to accurate and meaningful appraisal.

What is indicated by term?

"Too long," one writes on a paper where ideas are submerged in an avalanche of words, or "Too short," on another where brevity ceased to be a virtue.

Appraisal which is given in general terms such as those cited or others such as "Needs improving," "Poor," "Could be better" gives a student little insight into either the scope or nature of his accomplishments as viewed by the teacher or into the nature of the shortcomings needing correction. Terms indicating accomplishment need definition equally with terms indicating lack of the accomplishment desired. Such definition gives the student some understanding of how to appraise his own

Specific, not general

work. This is know-how which the youngest to the oldest student needs.

HAS THE ASSIGNMENT BEEN FULFILLED?

Helping a student know where he stands on his work involves helping him to see whether or not the assignment specified has been fulfilled. If not, where did he miss the point?

If it is an assignment calling for specified answers, it involves giving him the correct ones and checking or letting him check his work with them. This often raises the question as to the advisability of having students check one another's work rather than their own. This can get very personal. Further, the wrong person is making the appraisal. It is the student himself who is the one most concerned with his own work. But one may say it is hard for him to do it honestly and objectively. If so, that points directly to the greater need for learning how to do it. It suggests the possibility that one needs to help him turn his attention and turn one's own attention to the process of doing, rather than centering it on the end result. It is when the end result looms up as all-important that it may become difficult for a student to see beyond it to thinking how the work should be done and what can be gained from doing it.

Student is the one concerned

To Grade or Not to Grade?

Shall the homework be graded or not? Shall homework grades be counted in the final grade for the reporting period? If they are counted, what weight shall be given them? These are questions that go to the very root of the whole matter of homework and its fundamental purpose.

VALUE LIES IN THE DOING

The point has been made and maintained that the basic, fundamental, and valid reason for homework is to help the students in their learning. The value of the homework lies in the doing, in the practice it offers, in the knowledge it puts to work, in the thinking it stimulates, in the skills it develops and strengthens, in the opportunity it provides for independent use of varied abilities. Does a grade given for each piece of work tend to aid in achieving these purposes? Generally speaking, the answer is No. It tends rather to get in the way, to loom up with such importance that the student cannot see around it to the real good to be gained from the work to be done.

Grades often obscure purpose

The position has been taken emphatically that a student should know where he stands on his homework, but giving a grade is probably the least definitive of the ways of doing it.

HOMEWORK LEARNINGS SHOW UP IN CLASSROOM TESTS

In making a decision on grading homework think of it as preparation for classroom work. That puts it into proper perspective. There are plenty of classroom tests for arriving at grades. In the results of such tests the practice that homework offers becomes apparent; likewise the delving into knowledge, the gathering of information, the thinking and solving of problems, the observation of the neighborhood and community, and the reading assigned.

For example, an eighth-grade teacher was working with the students on public speaking. A homework assignment was given to prepare for a five-minute talk to be given in class. Several possible topics were listed. Students were told to prepare at home the main points they would bring out with supporting detail, to plan illustrations clarifying their points, and to prepare any exhibits they wanted to present as supplementary material.

The homework was distinctly preparation for the talks. The teacher did not grade the homework, though it was understood that the talks themselves would be graded. Prior to the final presentations, however, there was examination of the notes and outlines resulting from the homework and of any exhibits prepared. Some suggestions were made and help given, and a class period was spent in discussion of the points to be taken into account in the grading of the talks. This grading was done, not by the teacher in this instance, but by three persons from outside whom the students themselves had helped to select.

A teacher who undertakes to grade each piece of homework soon becomes so involved with variations of one point, one letter, a plus or a minus, that the purpose for which the homework exists is obscured to the point of disappearance.

A further factor pointing to the wisdom of not

Preparation for classroom work

Examined but not graded

Can become unduly involved

grading each piece of homework ties in with the complaint frequently heard from teachers that in the interest of a top grade parents do much of the work. An assignment done *for* a student works against him, since he does not have the preparation the homework is designed to provide. Grading that is done on the basis of classroom performance obviates this difficulty.

The situation is different when the preparation for some assignment is done in the classroom. The paper, report, or project to be produced then becomes the homework with the understanding that it *will* be graded. It is likely that this situation should occur more frequently as the students move into the upper grades and still more frequently as they enter high school with its greater departmentalization, larger classes, and less opportunity for individual and small group work.

Preparation done in the classroom

DON'T STUDENTS AND PARENTS WANT GRADES?

It is often maintained that if homework is not graded, students will become slipshod in doing it, that it takes the goad of a grade to keep them at it, that they cannot know where they stand without a grade. Further, it is often said that parents are not satisfied unless grades are forthcoming to indicate the effectiveness of the work.

Certainly parents want to know and have a right to know where the boy or girl stands, but thoughtful comments on papers such as have been indicated earlier in this chapter tell the story far better than a bare figure or letter and are a considerably

Comment more telling than a grade

healthier incentive than a grade given with the thought of its being a goad.

When homework, which has been thoughtfully planned, is examined and used in furthering classroom learning, experience shows that students tend to look upon it with respect and at least with a measure of acceptance. The very fact that it *is* examined and used bespeaks the importance the teacher attaches to it and lifts it in importance in their eyes. It becomes an impetus to effort. It speaks to the parents as well of the part it plays in the entire classroom situation. This leads to consideration of the part parents play in homework.

6

Working with the Parents on Homework

In Chapter 2 parents' varying attitudes toward homework were considered. The position was taken that whatever the attitude might be parents are necessarily a part of the homework picture, since homework enters into family living and affects the learning of their boys and girls. Further, the position was taken and is here reiterated that it is only as a teacher works with parents on homework that it can be expected to reach its optimum effectiveness. This raises the question of how to do it. Teachers will work with parents in individual ways, as they do all other phases of teaching. There are basic guidelines, however, that point to fundamental principles and are applicable to any situation.

Try to Get Their Point of View

An overall understanding of parents' thinking about homework is both desirable and useful but insufficient for arriving at a cooperative effort. The necessity remains to assess the points of view of the parents of each different group of students. The understanding of parents' attitudes is only background for the specific understanding of those in any immediate situation.

UTILIZE AND MAKE WAYS TO TALK WITH THEM

The only sure way for a teacher to arrive at an accurate understanding of how parents feel and think about homework is through direct contact with them. This means taking steps to establish such contacts.

Basic to finding the time to communicate with parents must come the realization of its importance and the willingness to explore ways of accomplishing it. From an understanding of parent attitudes can come significant cues for teaching. From parent help and cooperation can come support for the homework that has no counterpart in effectiveness. The contact may be made at some parent meeting, through a telephone call, during a casual meeting in the supermarket, or may be definitely planned for at home or elsewhere. There are always ways to do it, given the sense of urgency and the willingness to give time to accomplish it.

Worth the time

BE READY TO LISTEN

Listening is a fundamental necessity in discovering how parents feel about homework in general and their boy's or girl's in particular. Listening is a fine art. The more a teacher can do it without having neck bristles rise, the more likely parents are to feel free to speak their minds. The more one can listen without feeling complacent and self-satisfied about parents' favorable comments, the more one can learn from those comments. Further, the more one can listen without interrupting and the premature injection of one's own point of view, the broader and more complete the picture of parental thinking is likely to be.

Much gain

There is probably no greater test of a teacher's humility than the extent of the willingness to genuinely listen to parent comments. The time-honored assumption that it is the teacher's prerogative to *tell* rather than listen militates against doing more than politely waiting for the speaker to reach a period. Genuine listening implies the intent to hear perceptively. It is such listening that is essential if a teacher is to arrive at even a minimum of understanding of parental viewpoints on homework. With it one who is discerning will often become aware of feelings not yet expressed in words but potent in their influence and worthy of note.

Takes humility

GIVE HEED TO PARENT COMMENTS

Whether favorable or unfavorable, parent comments hold significance for teaching. In them lie cues to which a teacher does well to give heed. Those cues may be eminently useful in determining homework content, in planning, in assigning, in using. In any event, respect for parents and for their

Feel respect

right to their opinions bespeaks a respect for their comments that finds its expression in openminded consideration of them.

Some comments can be expected to be grumbles, and these merit attention, not merely defense of the assignment, but attention to see whether the grumble comes out of just cause. Sometimes it does, and the cause can be corrected profitably. Sometimes explanations clear away the difficulty. Anyway, every grumble best be given heed. Likewise the comments that are favorable.

Attend to complaints

A fifth-grade teacher who made a point of keeping in touch with parents received a phone call one evening from a mother who expressed appreciation for an assignment in homework that she and the father heartily approved. It was in social studies, and the students had been told to "Note and write down five inventions that make your living more comfortable and convenient than it would be if you did not have them." It led to a lively dinner table conversation with the parents telling how they were brought up without a lot of the things that the family was taking for granted. The mother said they were so glad to have homework sometimes that did not require poring over a book or going off into the boy's or girl's own room or nook to do it.

Attend to appreciation

Some other parents might have labeled such an assignment as silly and might have felt that it should have been more structured. A teacher who invites comments must be prepared for just such differences. But whatever the comments they should

Expect differences

be given heed. Not that one can follow all of them, but each has its own significance.

NOTE THE FAMILY-LIVING ASPECT

Homework is inevitably and inextricably interwoven with family living, with the fun, the chores, the eating, with the emergencies, the excitements, the worries and concerns, with the comings and goings, the disappointments, the rejoicings, with all that goes on.

"We never eat until late," a mother says to a teacher, "because my husband does not get home until late, and we all like to eat together, so he (the high school boy) has to get at his homework before supper and do the rest afterward. Sometimes he and his dad get to talking about a lot of things, and it is late before he gets at it, but it is about the only time he sees his dad, so that's how it is." Thus homework in that family must fit in with other things which that father and mother look upon as important.

In another home the mother tells how the kitchen table is the only place for homework to be done, and it is cleared the minute the evening meal is over so the four who have homework can get at it. She says, "We realize that they have to do it if they are to keep up with their classes." In some other home the story may be one of parents who pay little heed to whether the homework is done or not.

Whatever the situation may be, homework has a family-living aspect by virtue of the fact that it

Situations vary

goes into the homes and is done (or not done) in the midst of whatever the family living may be. This is something of which a teacher may well take cognizance. It is true that no teacher can know in detail the family living patterns of every home represented in any given classroom, nor the way those patterns and homework impinge on one another. However, there can be recognition of the fact that there is such impingement and that it is of vital significance for planning, for assessing results, and for consideration of individual guidance and assistance needed.

Home aspect significant

An important phase of trying to get the parents' point of view on homework in any given group is trying to come to an understanding of the way they see it as it relates to their family living. Even though homework cannot be tailored to fit all the differing conditions pertaining in any group, the very fact that a teacher is aware that there is a family living aspect to homework, is willing to consider it, and eager to understand it, is a factor in working with the parents on it.

Make It Easy for Parents to Cooperate

The suggestions outlined in the preceding section are steps toward making it easy for parents to cooperate in making homework effective. When carried out, they evidence a desire on the teacher's part to work with the parents. More than this, however, is needed. The more the teacher can do to make the desired cooperation easy to give, the more likely it is to be given.

SPEAK OF THE PURPOSE

The more clearly parents see the overall purposes of the homework given, the more clearly they are likely to relate themselves to it and the more easily they can make themselves a part of it. Obviously it is easier to cooperate when one knows what one is cooperating with than when one has little idea of what it is hoped to be accomplished and only a vague notion of the means by which it is proposed to be accomplished.

Why tell purpose?

This suggests speaking early in the year with parents, indeed at the very beginning, of the general purpose one sees homework serving in a particular group, such as assignments that will stimulate the students to think, that will help them to apply the knowledge they have, that will provide for drill and practice with meaning, that will call for thoughtful observation and the searching out of knowledge.

Explain general purpose

One may very well speak of the learnings inherent in homework other than specific subject matter, *e.g.*, the study habits formed, the responsibility taken for doing the work assigned, the satisfaction gained from putting forth honest effort, the independent recognition of work well-done.

It is reasonable to suppose that parents who understand such purposes underlying a teacher's assignments will find it easier to play their part in accomplishing those purposes than if they are left to

Makes sense to parents

guess at the reasons that lie in back of the work the students bring home.

The explanation of underlying purposes serves to provide the setting for day-to-day assignments. Understandably it serves to give parents confidence to know that definite purposefulness is the foundation for all of the homework given. It precludes the image of homework being used as busywork, a time filler, or as a method of punishment. When doubts and wonderings as to purpose are dispelled, cooperation is more readily given.

Begets confidence

EXPLAIN HOW HOMEWORK IS HANDLED

Useful as it is to speak to parents of the purposes of the homework, their understanding to be complete must include explanation of the daily planning that goes into it, of the way assignments are given, of the way the work done is examined and used.

Often a teacher thinks such details are of teacher rather than parent concern. They are indeed a part of teaching and therefore a teacher's responsibility, but they are also factors in the students' learning and so are of parent concern likewise. Information about the ways in which homework is presented and used gives them further basis for confidence and for understanding cooperation. Essentially it is a way of giving cooperation *to* the parents as well as making it easy for them to give their cooperation in accomplishing the teacher's purposes for the learning of their boys and girls.

Homework is also of parent concern

BE READY TO EXPLAIN

Obviously it is not possible to keep parents informed about each homework assignment, nor is it necessary to do so. The assignments, many of them, speak for themselves, once parents have the background of understanding the teacher's purposes and the nature of the homework in general. Likewise the students may help to explain the assignment but not always accurately. This is one reason for a teacher to be ready with explanations. Naturally students are closer to the homework and are less able than a teacher to see the overall picture.

Whether the explanation gives the reason for some particular assignment or clarifies the details of it or shows its place in a series to follow, the value of the explanation lies not only in the clarification but in the teacher's willingness to make it. It may be a general explanation to all parents or a particular one to individual parents whose boy or girl needs special help, or who have indicated interest in knowing more about the homework details than the student gives.

Willingness to explain is important

In any case the explanations a teacher gives directly to parents is one more step in making it easy for them to cooperate. It keeps them up-to-date on what is going on. It keeps lines of communication open and offers opportunity for such comments as they wish to make. Often a dittoed sheet giving the details of an assignment serves the purpose, or a word dropped at some casual meeting, or a telephone call if some special explaining seems in order.

WHEN POSSIBLE PUT ASSIGNMENTS INTO WRITING

The more a teacher can let parents know what is expected in homework, the easier it is for them to cooperate in getting it done. Putting assignments into writing is one useful way of informing them. It makes the assignment definite. It saves parents' questions and eliminates students' explanations which are often hazy and vague. Not that the students mean to be indefinite and not that they didn't listen when the assignment was given, but even with high school students, assignments have a way of slipping into the background in the lapse of time between hearing the assignment and getting at it at home. Details which sounded clear enough when the teacher was giving them have a way of becoming less clear when one tries to recall them.

Details become vague

An English teacher gave a second-year high school class an assignment to write an account of some experience occurring within the year which stood out to them individually as of unusual importance. Ten specific points were given as guides to the writing. These were thoroughly discussed in class. Students were told to take notes on the discussion. Presumably they did. The time came for doing the work at home, and the mother of one of the students gave a graphic account of the state of affairs as the student tried to decipher his notes and the parents tried to lend a hand in getting the work off the ground. A written assignment would have made their cooperation easier and more effective.

Student notes incomplete

"We are glad to help," said a father of four from fourth grade to twelfth, "but a lot of the time it's like working in the dark." It is a wise teacher who throws light for the parents on assignments. Putting homework into writing is one way of doing it.

Be Willing to Utilize Parent Help

Utilization of parent help in homework is predicated on teacher willingness to do so. Such willingness is not always present. Sometimes there seems to be the feeling that teacher prestige is in some measure diminished if one turns to parents for help, almost as if it were an admission of inadequacy. Often the complaint of not enough time accounts for the unwillingness; perhaps the uncertainty as to just how to use the help and the consequent reluctance to explore ways of doing it. Willingness to use parent help opens the way for increasing teaching effectiveness and for building relationships that bring benefit to all of the school-work.

SEE PARENTS AS INTERESTED

The basic assumption that parents are interested in the homework of their boys and girls is an approach that begets willingness to utilize such help. That very assumption tends to dispel the fear that they may be indifferent or outright averse to taking any part in it. With fear dispelled or lessened the reluctance to attempt to work with them naturally diminishes, and willingness to try to do so takes its

Dispel
fear

place. It is natural as one meets them here and there to speak of the homework, and once conversation is under way it is a short step to speaking of their part in it and of one's appreciation of their help.

The assumption of their interest is a valid one. It is their boy's or girl's learning which is involved. They want that learning to move along. It is natural that they should want a hand in helping it to do so. Even with those who seem indifferent it is safe to assume that there is a spark of interest overlaid, as it may be, with assertions that teaching is the teacher's business and that parents cannot and should not be expected to take part in it.

Parent interest natural

Such assertions had been made repeatedly by the father of an eighth grader whose teacher had consistently assumed parent interest and had evidenced not only willingness but eagerness for their help. It was an assignment in social studies that uncovered the interest which had been well hidden. The father had maintained that homework was a useless waste of time and that he would have no part in even seeing to it that his boy kept up with it. The result, according to the mother, was constant battles to get it done with the father's attitude serving as encouragement to the boy in evading the necessity for doing it.

Sometimes hidden

Then came the assignment for each student to observe his own behavior for one day and to bring in an account of specific incidents in which he (or she) (1) had been helpful to someone; (2) had observed some safety measure; (3) had shown respect for authority; (4) had acted on the basis of some value accepted as being important; (5) had assumed some home responsibility.

The assignment appealed to the father as being of practical usefulness, and he sent word to the teacher that it was the first time he had seen homework that made sense. It was a comment that to an understanding teacher bespoke an interest underlying the complaints and antagonism hitherto shown. Often antagonism does speak of interest, though it appears in negative expression.

May seem negative

Whatever the parent attitude may be or appear *not* to be, a sound starting point for a teacher's willingness to utilize their help is assuming them to be interested.

RESPECT THE HELP PARENTS CAN GIVE

Respect for the help parents can give with the homework is a natural corollary to willingness to utilize it. As a matter of fact respect for it is basic to willingness to use it.

Varied potential

Respect is enhanced manyfold when a teacher considers the possible range such help can cover, as represented in any given group. It implies an open-minded recognition of the possible usefulness of differing sorts of help and the growing recognition that every parent has potential help to offer and that all of it is potent.

As a teacher thus open-mindedly considers what parents have to offer, respect for that contribution is certain to grow as one notes such items as the provision of a place where work can be done; the

All of it important

encouragement to do the work; the adjustment of
family affairs so that it can be done; the time given
to prod the student into doing it when such prodding is necessary. This is help that should be duly
respected and by no means minimized in its importance nor written off as something to be taken
for granted. It is help deserving of great respect.
It is help that is significant not only because it sets
the conditions that make the doing of the work possible but because the very arrangement of those
conditions bespeaks the parents' recognition of
homework as important enough to provide for and
evidences an interest in doing so.

INVITE PARENT HELP

Inviting parent help goes one step beyond being
willing to use it and respecting it. It is actively seek-
ing it.

"Ask your father and/or your mother for an interview," a teacher directed a seventh-grade group.
"Ask them to tell you some of the things that were
done differently when they were your age." This is
using firsthand resource material available at home
for studying change in the ways of living. It is inviting help from parents and respecting the help
they can give. It is making such respect evident to
the students to whom the assignment is given.

A second-grade teacher who wanted to encourage
the children to do outside reading helped different
ones select simple books within their reading ability from the school library to take home. A note
had previously been sent home telling of the plan

An assign-
ment can
invite
help

for helping to get a library habit formed as well as broadening the scope of the children's reading and encouraging them to read outside of school. Parents were asked to listen to their boy or girl read the book. It was explained that a card would accompany each book which, if parent and child wished, the teacher would be glad to have the parents sign indicating that the book had been read to them. It was in no sense a checkup on either parents or child but a means of giving dignity and importance to a simple bit of beginning homework. It invited parent help and indicated plainly that such help was respected.

Assignments can show respect

It is easy enough, when a teacher wishes, to devise many assignments of varying sorts that thus utilize and invite parent help. It is one way to work with them on the homework. Not that one would expect to make every assignment of this kind, nor that one would expect parents to take a hand in every piece of homework that enters the house. There are many ways of working with the parents on homework, and it is a wise teacher who considers the possibilities and utilizes the help that is available in every home.

Valuable resource

KEEP IN COMMUNICATION

A two-way flow of communication—school to home, home to school—facilitates working together on homework. It is natural that this should be so. One cooperates more easily with that with which one is familiar.

This need be no arduous task of attempting to

talk with every parent at stated intervals nor of giving daily or even weekly information. The essence of this communication is the relationship which makes the give and take of information natural and easy, whether it be through casual conversation, by means of a dittoed sheet of explanation of some assignment, a telephone call, a home visit, an appointment at school, or some other way.

Knowing that the way is open *to* communicate is an essential element in communication and a salient factor in making it easy for parents to cooperate in making the homework effective.

Let Parents Know How to Help

In considering parent help in homework certain questions are sure to arise. What if such help is given in a way other than the way the teaching in the classroom is being done? What if the help given is confusing? Might it be better if it were not given? What about the possibilities of making the students dependent on home help? Is not the responsibility for homework theirs to carry independently? How much help has a teacher the right to ask from busy parents? How can a teacher find the time to bring parents into the homework picture? All of these are valid questions to consider.

IT IS TIME WELL-SPENT

Teaching time is precious. But when one considers the help which parents can give in homework, one can scarcely afford to take the time *not* to utilize it. Think of the impetus to effort that ensues on students' parts when parents and teacher work together. Think of the range of home resources and parent abilities that are represented in every classroom and that *can* be brought to bear on the homework given. Think of the time and effort turned to good purpose when mutual understanding takes the place of little understanding or misunderstanding.

Think of the advantages

It undeniably takes time to find the ways of working with parents on homework, as on anything else. How much more profitable, however, to spend the time thus than in using precious class time on material which could have been covered in homework! Homework is one of the most natural contacts a teacher can have with parents. It is the one phase of classroom work that goes into every home. It speaks to the parents of the way the teaching is being done. Working with the parents on it is the means by which a teacher can open the way for building relationships that can bring help into all the range of teaching. So considered, there is no time *not* to do it. But one does need to examine the ways of letting parents know how to help.

An entirely natural contact

EXPLAIN HOW THE TEACHING IS BEING DONE

It is in the teaching of arithmetic, reading, writing, and spelling that one most often hears of confusion arising from teaching done one way at school and parents' helping in another way at home. But this is no insurmountable obstacle. Parents are usually glad to know how the teaching is being done if the teacher is willing to go into detail about it.

Parents are glad to know

True, not all parents would be willing to come a few evenings for a couple of hours to hear explanations, but many would welcome the opportunity.

As students progress in the grades, it may be interesting to them to discover that there are ways of arriving at given results other than the way they are being taught, that this is the way that at present seems best but that there are others. Part of respect for parent help is respect for the fact that the ways they know of arriving at results in arithmetic, for example, may be perfectly good and useful ones. Instead of ignoring them or scorning them as outmoded, worthless, or obsolete, it gives the opportunity to show students that other ways have been substituted as learning has moved ahead. It can be eminently useful for students to understand that in education, as in all else, thinking progresses and methods change.

No scorn for other methods

It is not as if parents were to do the teaching at home. They are doing the *helping*. It is not that they will be developing new material with the students. This is done in the classroom. Nor do they need to know all the fine details of teaching. Rather, when they know the general trend which the teacher is following, they can give the lift here, ask the question there, point out the fact somewhere else that may be the bit of help the boy or girl needs to move ahead with the work assigned instead of floundering with it or giving up in despair.

Helping with understanding

There are plenty of ways that parents can help much more effectively than by actually getting into the detailed work of arithmetic problems or the work with phonics which the teacher may be using as a tool in teaching reading. They can do plenty to help other than getting into the details of the form for a story plot. It may be much more significant help if they talk with the boy or girl about the content of the story to be written than about the form it is to be put into. Similarly, it can be far greater help if parents listen to a child read and talk with him about the main points of what he has read than if they go into the details of how he is learning to do it.

Not all the details

GIVE SPECIFIC EXAMPLES OF WAYS THEY CAN HELP

It is helpful to parents when a teacher states in specific terms how they can be of help. By providing reference material is one of these ways. Not all parents can afford it, but many can. They are often glad to discuss what kinds of materials are most useful at the moment, and what kinds will last over a period of time as the boy or girl progresses in the grades. Another thing to talk about is their help in encouraging the boy or girl to search for resource material at the public library and in giving such assistance as needed.

Often it does not occur to parents that after their child has left the second or third grade it still is eminently helpful to continue reading to and with them. It surprises many parents to have a teacher suggest their reading to or with their sixth- or seventh-grade boy or girl, but reading is a skill that

Reading with boy or girl

touches all the student's schoolwork, and here is one way of helping to make sure there is accurate comprehension of what is read. Reading an arithmetic problem with a boy or girl is often all that is needed to make intelligible what seemed only so many words before. Reading a history assignment with discussion of main points as one goes along may be what is needed to make the words come alive and the main points stand out.

But, one may ask, is not this work a student is supposed to be doing independently? Yes, but sometimes, oftentimes, a lift is needed on the way, and parent help can give it. Sometimes the help needed is moral support, encouragement to keep at what is to be done, the word of commendation for the effort being put forth, the assurance that one knows they can do it. This is help of high order, that encourages a boy or girl to stick to what has to be done, to stretch to do it, to attack it with the thought that it *can* be done. It is help parents often do not think of as being of any significance because it is so natural to give it. It is help that they often think a teacher does not recognize as help. It is a good idea to let parents know that it is fully recognized and respected.

Different kinds of help

POINT OUT HOW FAMILY DISCUSSION
CAN BE AN AID

Seventh-grader Eric came home with the assignment to bring in four news headlines, either from the newspaper or heard on the radio or television, one each that referred to (1) world affairs; (2) United States affairs; (3) state affairs; (4) local affairs. The teacher had been working with the class not only on different types of news but also on headlines and how these are designed to attract attention and to give the kernel of the news in a few words.

There was great family discussion that evening as the boy went about picking out the headlines. Probably he could have done it without the discussion, for the teacher had developed the assignment clearly, and the boy knew what he was to do, but he did it better because of the discussion. The parents may not have realized how much help they were really giving both through their interest and through throwing ideas back and forth about the headlines that best fulfilled the assignment.

Natural interest

It is a good idea to let parents know that it is significant help when they do just the kind of thing Eric's parents did. It is not necessarily that the student cannot do the work without this help. Rather, he can often do it better *with* it. The very fact of talking with parents about an assignment brings ideas into focus with greater clarity, or opens up new viewpoints, or stimulates sharper thinking. Many times it surprises parents to hear that the teacher looks upon such discussion as helpful, and when they discover that it is so, they make more of a point of helping.

Discussion is stimulating

Parents of a high school girl in a homemaking class were astonished when the girl's teacher one evening at a PTA meeting took a moment to express appreciation of some help that they had given on a recent assignment. The parents, in telling of their appreciation of the teacher's comment, said it had never occurred to them that they were giving any special help. When the girl told about the assignment at home, it interested them, and they got to talking about it with no special thought of giving homework help. The mother said, "We just naturally talk things like that over because we are interested in what the children do, but as for helping with her homework that was farthest from our minds, but we did appreciate the teacher's speaking about it." Of course they did.

The assignment had been to think over ten relatives and friends you know well and then tell (1) how many different kinds of houses they live in; (2) what people there are in each family; (3) what they especially like to do for fun; (4) what pets they have.

The assignment had grown out of class discussions about how people live differently, how the makeup of the family differs, how different ones choose different kinds of houses. It was an assignment that lent itself easily to family discussion.

Notice that there was nothing in it that in any way pried into family living—just a look at some of the ways of living that no one would mind having looked at—and no invitation to criticism of any sort, but something to which parents could add many details the young person might have missed.

May be unaware that it is helpful

Parents can add details

And why shouldn't they? They are not doing the work *for* the student but are helping him in a very natural sort of way to do it and do it well. It is giving the support of interest that may lead one into a discussion that enriches.

URGE PARENTS TO ENCOURAGE INDEPENDENT WORK

Parent help that *does* the work instead of encouraging the student's independent doing of it is not genuine help. Homework at its best is an exercise in learning rather than the accomplishment of an end result, and the result is of importance only as it shows evidence of learning. Thus doing the work *for* the student becomes a hindrance rather than a help.

Not doing it for them

This possibility offers ample reason for talking with parents about *how* to help, ample reason for speaking specifically about the kind of help that makes a student independent in accomplishing the purpose of the homework.

It may be recalled that in discussing the matter of grading or not grading homework the point was made that when grading is done on the basis of classroom performance and achievement on tests, it penalizes a student to have had homework done *for* him. This is a significant point to clarify for parents.

It should be clear to parents that there is no expectation nor any desire that they should become actively involved with every piece of homework. It is rather that their general interest in and familiar-

Parent support adds dignity to homework

ity with it gives a needed support and dignity to it and sets it in its place in the family living as of importance.

It should be clear to the teacher that parents, too, are teachers, and every home is a learning laboratory. Herein is notable reason for working with them on the homework.

Conclusion

HOMEWORK should never be thought of as extraneous to teaching, but rather as an inherent part of it. Thus has it been presented here. It should never be considered as an isolated part of school living because it is done outside the classroom. It should be considered as inextricably interwoven with it, both growing out of it and becoming again fused with it as it is brought into active classroom use. It should never be thought of as in any way separated from the teaching done in the classroom. Homework is, in itself, a way of teaching for the teacher and a way of learning for the students. It should always be so considered. There remains then no question whether it should be done but only how it shall be done to fit each group of students in a way that best enhances their learning.

Index

Index